——— Pete Walsh MCC ———

COACH
TO WIN THE
LEADERSHIP
GAME

Accelerate team development and inspire
accountability to win in the marketplace

COACH TO WIN THE LEADERSHIP GAME

Copyright © 2010 by Pete Walsh

For information about this title or to order other books and/or electronic media, contact the publisher:
Peak Performance Coaching, LLC
4144 N. 44th Street Suite F
Phoenix, Arizona 85018
www.peakcoach.com
602-952-9015

ISBN: 978-0-9829493-0-6

Printed in the United States of America

First Printing: 2010

Cover and Interior design by: 1106 Design

Dedication

This book is dedicated to three people . . .

Loida Rike, one of the most important teachers in my life. Thank you, Loida, for that day in 1989 when you introduced me to the concept of professional coaching. In that moment you helped create an exciting new opening in my life and a big ripple in the universe. Since that day, I have been blessed to do my life's work and, in turn, have been able to impact hundreds of leaders and their organizations. You'll continue to be my coach every day of my life. I can feel your presence in every coaching session. Thank you for being who you are: the spirit, the leader and coach.

. . . And to Karen, my best friend, loving wife and life partner. Without your energy, spirit and support, none of this would have been possible. Thank you for your endless love and dedication to me, our family and our friends. Your love and devotion have empowered me to follow my calling and make a positive impact in the world.

. . . And to Margaret Walsh, my mother, my first coach and my friend, who from an early age, encouraged me, held me accountable, and taught me that I could become whoever I wanted to be. Thank you.

Contents

Foreword

Years ago, "Chief" George Miller described, quite simply, the purpose of The Boy Scouts of America. George, the longtime Chief Scout Executive of the Theodore Roosevelt Council BSA in Phoenix, Arizona, described scouting as, "A man and a boy sitting on a log exchanging knowledge and imparting direction in life."

That, quite simply, is what coaching is, whether it be in a classroom, an office, or a baseball diamond—converting experience to application. Too often we entangle ourselves in overly describing the simple act of coaching or, some may prefer, teaching.

Over seventeen hot Arizona summers it was my pleasure to coach 334 boys (prior to the entry of girls) in Little League, Senior League, and American Legion baseball teams. The players ranged from eight to eighteen, offering wide varieties of challenges, skills, fears, and opportunities.

One of my most memorable challenges was an awkward, gangly ten-year-old who, in baseball terminology, became a "project." His name was Pete—or as his mom Margaret called him—Peter Walsh. Over three seasons as his coach, I can say without reservation, nobody ever practiced harder or committed himself more to self-improvement than Pete.

By circumstance, Pete and his teammates, lovingly referred to as "The Bad News Bears," were assigned to me as "players" not selected by coaches in the draft. Our first year we won just one of eighteen games. Two seasons later, with the same nucleus of players, we won the division championship.

When he started playing, Pete Walsh had poor vision, limited coordination, and a weak frame. He also had an insatiable heart, and a determination that warranted/demanded special coaching. Pete and his teammates required and deserved extra practices, some "optional" on Sundays. Pete's motivation would sometimes try my patience. My assistant coach, a man who achieved considerable athletic success, taught Pete a level bat swing.

In this book, Pete recalls himself as a "decent" hitter. He became a very good #3 line-up hitter. The "other" coach who worked with Pete was Jerry Colangelo who achieved much success with the Phoenix Suns, Arizona Diamondbacks, and as Chairman of the United States' Olympic basketball champions.

Today, Pete Walsh has achieved career success as a business coach, author, husband, and father. He may be embarrassed by this assessment, but he is a model for maximizing one's talent.

Coach to Win the Leadership Game is not just a compilation of words, but a testament of one who dedicated himself to surpass limitations. Pete Walsh writes from the heart. The same heart he found on a dusty baseball diamond forty years ago.

—Bill Shover

Acknowledgments

I would like to acknowledge . . .

- Will and Laura, my friends and my coaches, who work with me to learn how to be a great dad.

- Jennifer, without your support and encouragement this wouldn't have turned out the way it turned out. Thank you for your patience, your courage, your humor, and your friendship. I thought your threat of "finish the book or I'll leave" was inspirational and bold!

- Clay, my very first professional coach. You showed me the way to be a courageous and bold coach. Your style made a quick and lasting impression on me as a coach.

- Mark, my second professional coach. Your wisdom, presence, and depth opened me up to new and powerful thinking and the development of my own presence as a coach.

- Donna, you have been my partner in coaching many leaders and organizations. Your knowledge, attention to detail, and commitment to client service has been invaluable to me and Peak Performance Coaching.

- Molly, your leadership catapulted me to new heights on so many levels. Thank you for continuing to show me the way.

- Park, your energy and friendship sparked this book to life at the cabin last summer. Thanks for being an inspiration as a businessman, husband, and father.

- Bill, my most influential coach and contributor to the beginning of my coaching legacy. The lessons I learned from you transcended baseball and have made a profound impact on my life.

- Pat and Bob, Mike and Mary, Rick and Jeff, for allowing me to really spread my wings as a coach in your organizations.

- Tim M., my friend and fellow entrepreneur, your consistent effort, focus and attention to detail inspires me to "keep pedaling" every day.

- Carl and Steven, the two guys who believed I could venture out and be a coach and helped push me off the ledge. Thanks, guys!

Introduction

Since 1980 I have been involved in the business world as an employee, then as a manager, and eventually an executive. From the very beginning it seemed like my bosses wanted more results from me, yet their way of trying to get more results were mostly cryptic, inconsistent, and ineffective. They wanted more results and I wanted more consistent and concrete help achieving those results.

Before long it was 1990 and I was a young executive. I found myself sitting at my desk, watching all of my employees happily walk out the door at the end of the day, despite having achieved only mediocre financial and customer satisfaction results, as compared to our stated goals.

It was an extremely frustrating feeling to see they lacked the personal ownership for results that we needed if we were going to be great in our business.

I started thinking about where I had seen individual ownership for results and team effort come together. I immediately thought about Bill Shover. Bill was my little league coach fifteen years earlier in the Arcadia Little League.

Bill had a tremendous influence in my life at a time when I had bad grades, bad teenage behavior, and no personal ownership for any of it. All of that would change as Bill stirred a sense of pride and possibility into my Little League baseball career.

Bill was a coach through and through. He knew how to teach, engage, and set a backdrop that made us want to stretch further and become something.

The question was, would the principles of coaching baseball players translate into business? In baseball, the goal was to have a plan to improve skills and be better than our opponents. So I thought, "*YES* the coaching principles may work!" In 1990 I began modeling my approach after Bill's, encouraging better performance, designing practice sessions that helped people develop new skills, which cultivated a sense of teamwork and a desire to reach higher levels of results.

Slowly I began to see people become more engaged and more committed to me and my message. They genuinely began to listen and showed signs of wanting to become better. They were willing to be accountable for their results. I was actually enjoying the challenge and intrigued by how to do more of it. I did not really realize it at the time, but I was becoming a *coaching leader.* I became enthralled in the process. Little did I know at the time this was going to become my life's work.

By 1998, as I saw the field of professional coaching emerging, I knew I wanted to be one of the people to define and prove the impact of this type of leading. I was blessed to have a wonderful friend, wife, and life partner who allowed me to follow my dream. In 1999, I left my job as vice president of a company, and became an executive coach.

Since then, I have had the privilege of coaching CEOs and leadership teams in some of the most respected companies in America from Bangor, Maine to Seattle, Washington. After coaching hundreds of leaders, I've seen a consistent pattern emerge—an overwhelming dissatisfaction with the level of results leaders are getting out of their staff! But what amazes me more than that is the lack of effort and attention that is actually given to learning how to grow and develop people! I believe coaching, and what I will call the language of coaching, and the *coaching leader* is the answer to solve this widespread dilemma.

Becoming a *coaching leader* gives leaders a reliable and predictable way to engage their staff, create personal ownership and responsibility, and enjoy the role of leader. Coaching, at its very core, is about building personal responsibility and accountability for results. This is the way to shift responsibility and energy from you as the frustrated leader, to your staff. Like me, that individual contributor thirty years ago, most of your staff is eager to be engaged in a different, more meaningful, and more effective way.

In fact, I fully believe that in the changing environment of the business world, coaching is now the best way to get great results and engagement from people. The spark that Bill Shover created in me and our team was palpable. Success in the field of business requires the same thing we had on that ball field—a high degree of personal dedication, a commitment to the process, a competitive spirit, and some fun.

So if you are a leader who is less than satisfied with the results your team is producing, I invite you to join me in this worthwhile and exciting adventure called the *coaching leader.* I promise that if you apply yourself and are consistent in your practice and approach, you will find a new sense of personal satisfaction and reward as well as team satisfaction and reward.

I have an additional offer for you. I would also like to coach you along the way. It is really the best way for you to experience the value of coaching. So if you are ready, let's get started!

—Pete Walsh

Bill Shover   Pete

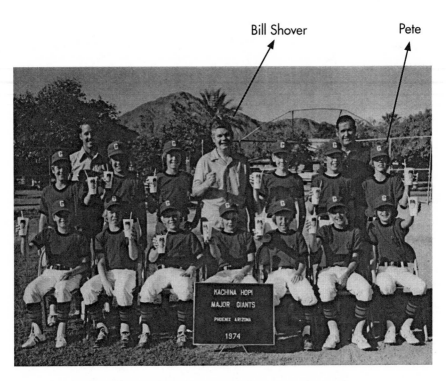

The original "Bad News Bears" were soon to be
impacted by a great *coaching leader!*

How to Use This Book

So many frustrated leaders—yet so little time spent trying to LEARN how to grow people and hold them ACCOUNTABLE to results!

Learning new skills and creating sustainable change in behavior requires *practice*. I would not be a great coach if I did not set the expectation of the importance of practice at the very beginning of this journey together. To say it another way, please read this book with the commitment and willingness to do the *practice* that great leadership requires.

I have a whole bookcase full of leadership books and you may too. But the bottom line as with everything, if you do not take the information and commit to integrating it into what you're doing, it really will not make any significant difference.

As long as we are on the subject of a bookshelf full of books, please bring a *beginner's mind* to this book. I know you are a successful leader, but as you read this book, pretend you *know nothing* about growing and developing people. That beginner's mind will allow you to be so much more coachable.

More than anything, I am committed to helping leaders become more *effective* in their businesses that will, in turn, create more rewarding and satisfying lives. I believe business is one of the most influential communities on the planet, and as leaders in business, we have an incredibly important role. If, as leaders, we can become more effective at *harnessing and utilizing human performance,* we can fulfill our company's missions and have a positive impact in the world. If you can be very effective at inspiring and bringing out potential and performance, I believe your team members will be more satisfied in their roles, and that will create a positive impact on their families, their communities, and the world. This is a very important role we play.

CHAPTER ONE

Why Coaching Now?

The End of Leadership

"The end of leadership" is a pretty bold statement. If you look around you will see some very dramatic changes in the world. I believe that our traditional leadership *structures* are falling away and a new form of leadership is emerging.

In fact, the genesis of this bold statement came from Warren Bennis, a pioneer in the field of contemporary leadership studies, in his article, *"The End of Leadership: Exemplary Leadership is Impossible Without the Full Inclusion, Initiatives, and Cooperation of Followers."* Bennis previously had been an advocate of TOPdown leadership. After being asked to debate against his TOPdown position, Bennis came to a startling conclusion. He writes, "I came to the unmistakable revelation that TOPdown leadership was not only wrong, unrealistic, and maladaptive, but also given the report of history, dangerous."

My experience as an executive coach brings me to the same conclusion. Leaders are struggling to connect with their workforce in a way that brings engagement, personal accountability, loyalty, and high levels of results. This lack of accountability for results is a very frustrating situation for leaders.

Our past beliefs, and subsequent strategies about leadership, are no longer relevant. There are a number of factors that have brought this about.

Failure of Leaders

Some of our most revered political leaders and corporate CEOs have been caught in outright lies that have undermined the credibility and trust we have traditionally bestowed upon them. These leadership failures have created a backdrop of *cynicism* and *doubt* amongst the broader group of followers.

"Pay Less, Get More" Mentality

The next factor is the extremely high expectation of consumers. As consumers, we expect high levels of deliverables from everywhere we exchange our time and money. With the advent of warehouse stores, major discounters selling everything, we expect to "pay less and get more." In fact, that is one of the most successful and popular marketing slogans in retail. This mindset spills over into the employee/employer relationship. People want to give less and be paid more. Deep down I would like to think that people are fair and are willing to have a fair exchange for their time for money, but they get caught in the cultural drift of a "give less, get more" mentality.

Get a Trophy for Just Showing Up

Let's layer on another dynamic. I do not know if you have raised children lately, but we started giving trophies just for *participating* on a team. This new *cultural norm* has created an expectation of reward and recognition for just showing up. There are bodies of research now revealing that this may not be the best approach in terms of teaching young people how to work hard and achieve something. Parents are afraid to let their children feel anything other than "success" and they have no idea how to deal with adversity or disappointments that might come their way as adults. They expect to be promoted to vice president within a couple of years after graduating from college.

People Want More Satisfaction and Meaning

In a recent poll by the Conference Board, the ninety-year-old business research organization, it appears that job satisfaction is at an all time low. This is another indication that our current forms of leadership are not creating work environments that have people satisfied and engaged.

As we look at the *cultural context* of leadership today, we see a shift occurring in the employee-employer relationship. Cultural context is the background of experiences and beliefs that are shaping our collective thinking. This is the cultural context in which business is done today. We have four dynamics:

- Cynicism due to major leadership failures;
- Give less, be paid more mentality;
- Reward and recognition for just showing up; and
- People want more satisfaction and meaning.

How easy it must have been in the days of leadership fifty years ago! "Work hard, don't complain and you're lucky to have a job." Well, ladies and gentleman, we are not in Kansas anymore.

So, it is really not the end of leadership, but leadership as we know it is no longer effective. So, what type of leadership is best suited for today's business world?

Opportunity for a New Form of Leadership

By now we have a clearer picture about the world in which we lead. In every crisis is an opportunity. People are looking for teachers and a beacon of light in this tumultuous world. Leaders who can understand this opportunity and adjust to a new form of leadership will create the most competitively vibrant teams and financially successful organizations. Throughout this book you will learn about the **coaching leader.** This new form of leader knows how to inspire, engage, and hold people accountable to higher levels of performance and business results. But more importantly, in the coaching and development process, both leaders and team members experience a much higher level of personal satisfaction and reward for their work. Coaching is deeply rooted in helping people understand their true talents, gifts, and how to use those to reach their *potential.* This new form of leadership will create higher business results and greater levels of personal satisfaction for you and your team's needs.

Competitive World

It is a competitive world. Just look around; you see new organizations popping up all of the time, and at the same time you see old stalwarts like General Motors, that we thought were unbeatable, falling to the wayside. It is an extremely competitive world. Survival of the fittest is really what it comes down to in our economic system. Believing that there is room for charity or keeping organizations around for sentimental value is unrealistic. Only the most effective, competitive, and profitable organizations will succeed. The sooner we understand this as leaders, and the sooner we can convey this message to our staff in a way that they can hear it, the better off we are all going to be.

Average equals extinction is reality. Think about it; if you are only maintaining the status quo, you are probably not going to survive. So the challenge from a leadership perspective is to continually have your organization *staying ahead* of the pack.

How do you do that? Here is why coaching is so critically important. Coaching focuses on performance, improvement, and potential. Getting better and higher levels of performance really isn't an option anymore; it is the only option! I am not saying that the highly competitive world is the right world, but it is the world we live in as business leaders today. To deny that reality would be poor business strategy.

You would be better off to understand that this is the world we are in; the sooner you can create a highly effective and competitive team, the sooner you are going to enjoy success, profitability, loyalty, and retention.

Coaching Embraces Transparency and Access to Information

Look at the media, Internet, etc. We pretty much know all there is to know about everybody. Facebook, Twitter, LinkedIn; it's all right there to see. Part of the story that a *coaching leader* conveys is that there are no secrets. *Coaching leaders* say, "Let's get our performance out in the open so we can see it, be accountable, and find ways to improve it." One of the cornerstones of a great *coaching leader's* organization is that everyone is accountable for their piece of the puzzle and we can all see each other's pieces. Not that we want to make anyone wrong or find blame; on the contrary, if we are going to be a great team it is critical that we all know what everyone else is doing.

Coaching is an *accelerator* for learning and development. If it is, in fact, a very competitive world, and we must continue to get better, then we must find the best tool to help us get better. That tool is coaching. Coaching is all about:

- Accelerating development,
- Holding people accountable for results, and
- Winning in the marketplace.

Technology and systems are important, but the most important resource in an organization is human capital. It is one of the resources that is the trickiest to impact and again why coaching is so critically important.

Who is Your Bill Shover?

Bill Shover is the coach and central character in this story who made an indelible mark on my life. In fact, he is still an important influence. The truth is, when I was a twelve-year-old and met Bill, I was not in a great personal situation. My father had serious personal challenges and was pretty much out of the picture. I did not have a lot of reasons to be confident in who I was, although from an early age I was mesmerized by sports and spent hours in the front yard shooting hoops and imagining that I was making the final shot to win the NBA championship.

Bill Shover took me under his wing in the Kachina Little League in 1974. I got a sense pretty quickly that Bill had a *process* for what he was doing, a great spirit about what he was up to, and a real compassion for the underachiever. I really felt like I was fortunate to be picked for his team.

Bill was encouraging and compassionate from the very beginning. His coaching approach was about working on the *fundamentals* and understanding the game. This approach instilled a certain amount of confidence because we kept repeating the fundamentals.

When Bill and I met recently, (thirty years after being coached by him in Little League), he recounted this story. He said, "When I started working with you, you were really not a very good hitter, but if you remember, we kept working and working on the fundamentals and eventually you began to get the bat on the ball and get them into the outfield for some very nice base hits. You really became a good hitter!"

He also shared that he was coaching his older son in American Legion ball at the time and that he was arm-twisted into taking a team in the minor leagues. Here I thought I had been so blessed to be picked by Bill Shover, but the truth of the matter was he got a minor league team with the bottom of the barrel players (the early version of the Bad News Bears). Luckily his son, T.A., was a good ballplayer and Bill knew how to make ballplayers out of young boys who were a little lacking in the talent department.

That was an important step in my life. Through his patience, encouragement, support, and *process* of practicing the fundamentals, I did in fact become a decent hitter.

A really great thing about Bill and his process was that he knew how to have fun. This is something I have carried through into my life and my executive coaching. When we have fun, or lightness as I like to call it, we tend to be better learners and are free to bring out our natural energy and talent.

Early on, Bill made it very clear that he was about playing players who worked hard. This was an expression of one of his values, a critical piece of coaching. I knew if I showed up at practice, worked hard, and applied myself, Bill was going to give me my fair share of playing time and perhaps start me, even though I probably was not at the top of the talent list. Bill rewarded hard work and determination.

All of this led to a greater sense of self-worth from my perspective. It felt good to have a champion like Bill rooting for me in my corner. He would cheer any time we did something right. He would also make sure to point out if we missed the mark. This is another hallmark of a great coach. They are attentive to details, both the positive details and the details for areas with room for improvement.

I was fortunate enough to have Bill draft me in a second and third season. By now he knew my commitment to improvement and I knew his system. I was a loyal fan, and he was a devoted coach, helping me improve my baseball skills and personal confidence.

When Bill and I had lunch recently, he said to me, "I had 334 kids and not one of them tried harder than you." Imagine how great that felt! Here he is in his seventies; I am in my forties and he is still coaching me and contributing in a very positive way. What a special relationship.

A Partnership Like No Other

Coaching is a very unique and special *partnership*. As a manager, people know that you are fundamentally trying to get them to be in compliance and produce certain results. But, as a coach, there tends to be more of a feeling of partnership toward your mutual success and development. That partnership creates a different energy and willingness to be open to new ways of looking at things and being taught. That new energy is usually based upon *trust* and is the foundation for the whole coaching relationship. When a manager shifts his or her energy to that of a coach, it can make all the difference in the world.

Tapping into Renewable Energy

Tamara Woodbury, the CEO of Girl Scouts, Cactus Pine Council, says, "One of our greatest sources of renewable energy is the human spirit."

As the *coaching leader*, that is the energy you are trying to tap into! Have you noticed how on workdays we tend to hit the snooze button twice and drag ourselves out of bed to go to work? On weekends, we just jump out of bed and get going toward something we love to do.

What difference would it make in your business if people came to work with that kind of energy every day? That is the kind of energy that is available and can be brought out by a great coach. The mission of coaching is to help people uncover what matters most to them and identify their greatest strengths.

When you learn what matters most to people, you begin to tap into a new level of energy that is not often found in the work setting. Couple that energy with a higher degree of personal accountability and a clearer focus on results, and you begin to get a sense of what coaching can bring you as a leader.

As people get clear about what is most important to them, and what their greatest gifts are, one possible result is they decide they are on the wrong team or in the wrong position. As a leader running a business, it is better to have people who are fully committed and engaged in what they are doing.

Most people are not in this state of renewable energy; they are in various states of sleep walking, resentment, and discouragement. This energy has incredible productivity and morale value to corporate America every day. Coaching can tap into this renewable energy.

"Listen In": Shift in Energy When You Start Being Their Coach

Let's listen in to my coaching conversation with a senior executive at a large utility company early in my coaching career. I was developing my thinking about how, when leaders transition to become *coaching leaders,* it would impact their relationships with their direct reports.

LISTEN IN

Coach Pete: "So it sounds like you know Mary is capable of more, yet she doesn't seem open to your suggestions. Is that correct?

Client: "Yeah, she seems a bit defensive whenever we try to discuss some of her performance gaps."

Coach Pete: "Have you ever asked her point-blank if you could 'coach her?'"

Client: "I have been trying to work with her with a coaching style, but I've never actually asked her if I could coach her."

Coach Pete: "Would you be willing to make that explicit request of her? I would be interested to see what happens when you do that."

Client: "Okay, I'll ask her in our one-on-one meeting next week."

At our next coaching session:

Coach Pete: "Did you ask Mary if you could coach her?"

Client: "I did."

Coach Pete: "What happened?"

Client: "It was almost like the whole energy in the room shifted. It was like all of the sudden she (client's direct report), was listening to me from a whole different place. It was like suddenly she became more open to what I had to say and receptive to new ways of approaching things."

That lesson hit me right between the eyes and reinforced what I had instinctually believed. When she was able to explicitly call out a different relationship with her direct report, it created different energy, different openness, and different results. That is what is possible with coaching.

Lou Holtz on "Why Coaching"

Lou Holtz, the famous Notre Dame football coach, did a wonderful job of answering the "why coaching" question:

He writes, "Coaching gives one a chance to be *successful* as well as *significant*. The difference between those two is that when you die, your success comes to an end. When you are significant, you continue to help others be successful long after you are gone. Significance lasts many lifetimes. That is why people teach, people lead, and why people coach. As I leave the field of play, I enjoy the feeling of being a winning coach. But more important, I hope that I have been a person of significance in the lives of those young men."

Coaching creates a stronger and deeper connection to people and their willingness to work hard and stretch for extraordinary levels of business results. But, as Coach Holtz says, "Even more important is that I believe the impact you have as a *coaching leader* runs deeper and wider into how people live their lives, and in turn, impact others."

COACH THE COACH

Set aside fifteen to thirty minutes and reflect upon your beliefs and assumptions about leadership in business today.

- Does what I have written resonate about the need for a new form of leadership?
- Who have been the most influential leaders in your life and why?
- Do you believe coaching is an appropriate form of leadership today? Why or why not?

After reviewing your reflections, how might your thinking influence your ability to become a *coaching leader*? Are there any new perspectives about leadership that you should begin to practice?

CHAPTER TWO

Do You Have What It Takes to Be a Coaching Leader?

Now you can see the cultural forces at play, and the marketplace dynamics that are *demanding* more from you as a leader. The question becomes, "Do you have what it takes to be a *coaching leader?*"

Coaching—The Perfect Combination of Two Energies

Tamara Woodbury speaks about the "masculine and feminine archetypes" and the need in the business world to find the best of both of those types. I believe the *coaching leader* is the perfect combination of the two.

While there are various interpretations of the male and female archetypes, I like to boil it down to a simple comparison. The masculine archetype is typically about conquering and dominating. The feminine archetype is about nurturing, sustainability and community.

Coaching leaders are strong and demanding, yet want to see their team members grow, thrive and reach their potential. The *coaching leader* has an almost parental relationship with their coachees. (For the rest of the book I will use the term "coachee" for the person who is receiving the coaching.)

The 20 Qualities of a Coaching Leader

As a business leader and an executive coach for more than twenty-five years, I have found there are twenty qualities that emerge as the most critically important to be an effective *coaching leader*.

As you review each of these qualities, think about whether or not the quality is:

- An inherent strength (comes naturally to you);
- A quality you possess (but have had to learn); or
- A quality you need to develop (not present yet).

As your coach, I believe you can develop any of these qualities. I also believe that you will need to be aware and *practice* all of these qualities to achieve greatness.

1. Genuine Care for Others

People are not going to stretch, nor are they going to go the extra mile, unless they really believe that you care about them. Remember the old saying, "People don't care about how much you know, until they know how much you care!" This is so true in coaching. As we get into the tools and techniques of coaching, if you do not have a genuine care for others, people are not going to give you their best effort.

2. Passion to Grow People

At the core of great coaching is a fundamental desire to help people grow. *Coaching leaders* derive a real sense of *pride* and *accomplishment* when their team members overcome obstacles, master skills, and succeed.

If for any reason you are simply trying to get the most out of people to make money, I would suggest that coaching is not the right leadership approach for you. I believe that when we help people grow and produce at a high level, the financial success will follow.

3. Good Instincts About What Motivates People

One of a coach's greatest qualities is good instincts about people. What motivates them, inspires them, and makes them tick? Great *coaching leaders* have an uncanny and almost intuitive way of knowing what makes people tick. Part of the way they understand what motivates people is by taking time to get to know them, ask questions, and uncover their desires and ambitions. They know when to use that information in just the right moment to create outstanding results.

Vince Lombardi, the legendary football coach of the Green Bay Packers for eight years, was a master at this. One of his players, Jerry Kramer, an All-Star guard, tells the following story:

In one of the practice sessions early in his career, Kramer missed his blocking assignment on a play. On the very next play he jumped offside. He said, "Lombardi really jumped on me and reamed me out; he had me feeling awful! I felt like smacking him in the mouth!

"I was in the locker room after practice, ready to hang it up and do something else. Vince came up to me and patted me on the back and said, 'Son, don't you know that someday you'll be the best guard in this league?' **Those words lit a fire!**"

This little vignette is a great lesson for aspiring *coaching leaders.* Lombardi knew at that moment on the field that Kramer needed a swift kick in the pants. He also had the instinct to know that Kramer was in need of a pat on the back in the locker room.

Had Vince Lombardi not had that intuition about Jerry Kramer, one of the greatest guards of all time may have gone down a different road!

4. Ability to Build and Maintain Trust

Trust is where "the rubber meets the road" in coaching. It is very similar to how much you care about people. But if people do not trust you they are not going to listen to you, and they will not have a willingness to go "all out" to stretch themselves. Great *coaching leaders* establish long-term relationships built on trust. Trust is built through being your word, having actions aligned with stated values, and being impeccable about all that you do.

The delicate thing about trust is that it can take years to build and seconds to destroy. Trust is like the capital you have built that you use every day to run your business. Without trust, you are done, so be very careful about protecting it!

Remember the cultural context of cynicism for leaders. John Q. Public has been burned a time or two, so I encourage everyone to be impeccable as a *coaching leader.* If you happen to trip and make a mistake, clean it up quickly and be honest about it.

5. Produces High Levels of Personal Results

There is something I have always believed: you cannot teach what you do not know. In coaching, as in most things in life, if you are unable to personally produce a high level of results, those around you are not going to have great respect for you as a coach or as a leader. That does not mean that you have to produce the same type of results and the same type of work that those you are coaching produce, but you do have to produce at a high level in the things you are responsible for. You need to be able to model high-level performance if you are going to ask for it from others. If you were previously a high-level producer in the type of work that the people you are coaching do, that is even better, but not essential. The bottom line is you've got to be able to produce at a high level to garner the respect of the people you are coaching.

6. Has a Strong Achievement Drive

Great coaches are great pace setters. They are the ones who want it as much or more than anyone on the team. That kind of energy is contagious! The drive for excellence shows up in everything they do. Great *coaching leaders* are rarely distracted or discouraged in the face of adversity. They lead by example in terms of their own willingness to continually stretch themselves and their team. I think one of the great bonuses of being a *coaching leader* is that you always get to be holding the mirror up and working on yourself as well. For some of you that may not be very appealing! The bottom line is that great *coaching leaders* have an unending desire to get better, and they know that the quickest way to ruin a coaching relationship is to not practice what they preach.

That is not to say that you cannot show your faults. Transparency is a very important and endearing quality of great coaches. It is not to say that you are not going to have a breakdown or letdown occasionally. How you handle them will be very critical to your success, and will show determination and commitment to the vision at all times. Just be real; you can have faults.

So when I say, "working on you," I am not saying that you have to be perfect, but you should expect of yourself what you expect of your teammates. Those expectations may be hard work, determination, focus, and professionalism.

If you are going to have a coaching culture and be a *coaching leader,* I would suggest that you engage in a formal coaching relationship. One of the best insights I received in my career was from a mentor, Larry Snead. He told me, "The organization mirrors the leaders." As a coach, your team is only going to be as good as you are. You are the center spoke of a wider wheel, so keep working on you.

Consider getting your own coach to help you work on you, and also consider giving others in your organization permission to coach you. Your humanness and transparency will be one of the greatest ways to endear yourself to your team and build a high level of respect for you.

7. Emotional Intelligence

Great *coaching leaders* develop strong emotional intelligence. They know that reading people, connecting, and maintaining healthy relationship energy is the key to trust, commitment, and high-level performance.

In his groundbreaking research, Daniel Goleman proves that emotional intelligence can be developed and learned. Specifically, two competencies are critical to the *coaching leaders. Empathy* is about being able to connect with others and understand their concerns and motivators. *Nurturing relationships* is being able to develop meaningful and emotionally rewarding relationships that endure over time. If you want to be a successful *coaching leader,* you will develop these two competencies along with the other three competencies: emotional self-regulation, emotional motivation, and emotional awareness.

8. Strong Communication Skills

Communication skills are at the heart of great coaching. Great *coaching leaders* have the ability to convey not only the big picture vision, but also the minute details of techniques.

Communication skills obviously are critical in relation to creating accountability and drive for excellence. *Coaching leaders* are constantly reinforcing key messages that focus energy and effort on winning in the marketplace.

Communication skills include being a good listener. *Coaching leaders* are constantly listening to their team members and the team energy overall as they develop and decide upon the right messages to help their team succeed.

9. Ability to Articulate a Clear, Compelling Vision

A great *coaching leader* creates a clear and compelling vision that inspires unprecedented levels of creativity and performance.

They know the power of words and use them masterfully to declare new and bold futures for the team.

Take President John F. Kennedy's famous declaration, "We will put a man on the moon by the end of the decade," as a powerful example. Many who were involved later confessed, "we had no idea how we were going to get it done, but we somehow rose to his challenge." Great coaching leaders create compelling visions that inspire their teams.

10. Know How to Hold People Accountable

Great *coaching leaders* know how to hold people accountable in a way that is firm, yet fair, though not unreasonable and demanding. You get the picture? If we are going to achieve high results then we obviously have to be very good at creating accountability.

Troy Aikman, the former quarterback of the Dallas Cowboys, tells a great story about Coach Jimmy Johnson's ability to hold people accountable. After winning their first playoff game in years, Aikman was detained by jubilant reporters. Coach Johnson, realizing that the team's star performer was not on the bus on time, instructed the driver to leave the stadium. Aikman said that he was never late for the bus again.

11. Always Come from a Coaching Mindset

A coaching mindset is always resilient, optimistic, and looking to close the gaps needed for a higher-level performance. If you listen to great coaches, the lens they look through is always about what went well and what can improve. It is usually a balance between those two and never too one-sided. A coach knows that you should never think that you have reached perfection, but at the same time, if you are too critical and negative you will not foster confidence and determination.

12. Ability to Be Consistent

Consistency is going to be a key contributor to both trust and high levels of results. The bottom line is that excellence comes through consistency. Consistency in your word, energy, attention to detail, and focus on results are essential to being a *coaching leader.* You've got to be consistent if you are going to produce high results.

John Wooden, head coach of the UCLA men's basketball team and one of the most respected and successful coaches of the twentieth century, was known for his impeccable consistency about every aspect of the team's practice and game preparation. Wooden's teams won an unprecedented ten national championships over a twelve-year span.

13. Healthy Amount of Ego and Humility

Great *coaching leaders* already have their ego needs met from other places; they have a healthy amount of ego. To say it another way, they want to succeed, but at the same time, they are not caught up in their own gratification. They have reached a point in their careers where they are motivated by something bigger than themselves.

Bill Shover was one of the more high profile, widely known and respected business leaders in our community, yet when he walked on the field and became our coach he was down to earth, approachable, and humble; he gave us all room to be ourselves and be open to the coaching. I know he possessed a strong desire for us to succeed and felt a personal vested interest, but his even-keeled, comfortable style set a great tone in the dugout.

14. Patience

Great *coaching leaders* are patient when they need to be. They are patient when they see people with potential working hard, doing the right things, and striving to improve. They know excellence and mastery takes time and effort. They are willing to invest the time, energy, and patience into those individuals who show a genuine commitment to the process and possess the qualities they are looking for in the other members of the team.

15. Resilience

Great *coaching leaders* have the ability to stay positive in the face of adversity and failure. This is another way they set the tone for the team. If you think about the old adage, "If you can believe it, you can achieve it," imagine how important it is to keep a positive attitude in today's challenging and dynamic marketplace.

One of the best examples of this is the 2008 Super Bowl. The Arizona Cardinals scored an electrifying go-ahead touchdown by their star receiver, Larry Fitzgerald, with 2:39 left in the game. The Cardinals' defense had stopped the Steelers' offense for most of the second half, so it seemed like the Steelers might be defeated.

In the film of the game you see Coach Mike Tomlin very confidently say, "Let's go, it's our time to win this!" Upon reflection later, quarterback Ben Roethlisberger said that Tomlin's seemingly unfazed demeanor carried over to him, and in turn went into the huddle, where Ben challenged his teammates to rise to the occasion to prove they were the better team. How important was it that Tomlin was unfazed? What would have happened if the quarterback saw doubt or concern in his coach's eyes?

16. Ability to See With an Objective Eye

At the heart of coaching is performance improvement. Performance improvement requires good technique and attention to detail. *Coaching leaders* can see performance with an objective eye, being able to discern the nuances of great performance. Seeing with an objective eye is being able to suspend personal biases, either good or bad, and see the performance without the "story." You need to be able to break it down piece by piece, dissect it, and look for ways to improve.

Bill Belichick, the great coach for the New England Patriots, made his name in the coaching profession for his ability to see details that others could not see. His objective eye enabled him to analyze not only his team, but the other team's performance tendencies. Seeing this way gave him access to information that other's could not see and ultimately became his competitive advantage.

17. Embody Lightness When Needed

Another great quality for coaching is lightness. When a coach can bring lightness along with all of these other qualities, it can create a good environment for learning and development. If you think about it, most people find it difficult to learn when they feel immense pressure to perform. The art of lightness is the ability to be able to hold two opposing energies like strong achievement drive and lightheartedness at the same time.

There is a time and place for lightness of course, and great *coaching leaders* know the right time to use it.

18. Ability to Be Innovative and Creative

When we study many of the greatest coaches, we see that they were pioneers in the way they approached their craft. Lee Strasberg made actors go to deep dark places within themselves to find their voice. Bill Walsh of the San Francisco Forty-Niners, National Football League, invented a fast and short passing style that revolutionized the game and became known as "The West Coast Offense."

Great *coaching leaders* are not afraid to blaze a new trail in their profession; in fact, they see it as a big part of who they are. For some, this innovation is a result of one of their other qualities, such as drive for achievement or resilience. Any way you get there, you might think about your level of innovation and creativity.

19. Creates Great Teams of Assistant Coaches

Great *coaching leaders* not only build great teams of performers, they build a great team of assistant coaches. In many cases the assistants go on to become great coaches in their own right.

A cohesive team of assistant coaches allows great *coaching leaders* to leverage their process and build deeper and stronger organizations.

Bill Shover modeled this impeccably. Each year, even though he might be working with new assistant coaches, volunteer fathers, and friends, the players enjoyed consistent styles and approaches due to Bill's excellent leadership.

Of course, not every assistant coach scenario worked perfectly. On one warm afternoon Bill invited Jerry Colangelo, the coach of the Phoenix Suns, to come throw batting practice. Having a local sports hero pitching to us was a thrill, especially at age twelve.

Jerry appeared to be a talented hurler, except for one small problem. As each left-handed hitter came up, he proceeded to hit him with a pitch. By the time I came up to bat, as a lefty, I was shaking in terror expecting to be hit. Sure enough, six pitches later, a fastball struck me squarely on the elbow and sent me to the dirt writhing in pain. As it turned out, it was worth the pain because Bill and I have enjoyed retelling the story to this day!

20. Ability to Articulate and Model the Values

Great *coaching leaders* know the importance of clearly articulated and practiced values. The values act as a compass for both leadership and team behaviors and norms.

In 2001 when The Phoenix Suns' Jason Kidd was involved in domestic violence, Suns owner Jerry Colangelo had a dilemma. Kidd was one of the team's most potent weapons, but he also was a direct contradiction to the Suns' stated values of family and community.

At the end of the season, Colangelo did the unthinkable and traded Kidd. The trade created a bit of short-term panic for fans, but in the end an even stronger and more loyal fan base because Mr. Colangelo was willing to make that decision. That sent quite a message to the remaining players.

COACH THE COACH

- Go online at www.peakcoach.com and take the *coaching leader* online assessment.
- Identify two to four top gaps you would like to work on in relation to the twenty qualities of the *coaching leader.*
- Identify one to two new practices (skills, attitudes, behaviors) that you need to begin to utilize in order to close your gaps.

CHAPTER THREE

The How of Coaching

First, the 5,000-Foot View

Coaching is 50% science and 50% art. This chapter is a brief overview of the coaching system that I have developed over the past ten years. I want to give you the 5,000-foot view of the system so that you can see it from a high level before we dive in to the detail in subsequent chapters.

The Coaching *Conversation*

Most of the coaching you will be learning about in this book will take place in a coaching *conversation*. The coaching conversation has a certain feel and flow to it. A good coaching conversation has a *back and forth movement* that has to be *fluid* to be effective. Some conversations are short and sweet, some will take longer to unfold, or some may be a series of conversations over several months or years.

After many years of engaging in these types of conversations, I have identified four distinct *phases* of the conversation that must occur to achieve a strong outcome.

The PACE™ Coaching Process

I invented the PACE™ process with several things in mind. We have talked about the power of words and I thought that the acronym PACE™ was a great word play on the idea of consistent effort over a long period of time to achieve a result. PACE™ is simple in its approach and "sticky," in that it is easy to remember. I have both attended and taught coaching classes since 1998 and have experienced many variations of coaching models, but I have found, as have my clients, that simple and memorable is the most useful. The purpose of this book is to give business leaders a *simple* and *practical* method for coaching. If at some point you have an aspiration to become a professional coach, I would encourage you to embark on more sophisticated and elaborate coaching training that would further deepen and broaden your coaching knowledge.

Step 1: P for Perceived Need—a.k.a. "The Stuff That Drives Most Leaders Nuts!"

If you remember the starting point, the central character was trying to find a way for his staff to be more productive and produce higher levels of results. It seems only fitting that the first step in the coaching process is being able to identify the difference between the results you are currently seeing from your team members and *the results you think you should be getting.* In coaching we call that a **gap.**

So let's bring this down to real life, real business. Here are the most common gaps that show up for business leaders:

- Poor or substandard performance (sales, revenue, production)
- Breakdowns of one form or another—customer service, communication, etc.
- Developmental needs—someone not living up to their potential

- Unacceptable behavior or attitude
- Inappropriate mood or mindset

Without a Perceived Need, There is No Coaching

One of my favorite teachers, Julio Olalla, says that if there is no perceived need, there is no coaching. Your first step is to get your team members to see the same thing that you see in terms of the gap. It sounds simple and fundamental, but truthfully, there are some team members that tend to be stubborn, blind, and "play dumb" as strategies to avoid being held accountable to the gap in performance.

So as *coaching leaders* in this first step, one of the things we will do is get agreement with the coachee that there is, in fact, a gap and we are going to work on it together with the coaching mindset.

Step 2: A for Analysis—The "Choices" We Have in Front of Us

After we have agreed upon the gap, it is the coach's job to help the coachee think about the different options in terms of closing the gap. Remember *choice* is one of the bedrocks of coaching and empowering people to really buy into what they are doing. The old form of leadership (manager) simply would *tell the team member how to close the gap*. You can do this, but it won't create genuine buy-in, engagement, and **ownership of the results.**

Seeing the Patterns—The Opening for Real Change and Transformation

Part of the value of coaching is to simply begin to be aware of your patterns of behaviors and your *automatic ways of doing things.* Brain scientists are doing remarkable research on what "pattern makers" we are as human beings. The way they tell the story is that the brain "hardwires" as much as it possibly can to leave available memory and resources to process new information. A recent client used the phrase "cow paths" as a way of describing how her team members were simply following the path they had been following for many years. Step two of the coaching process is really about *interrupting the patterns* and empowering the coachee to see new options. We are actually trying to abruptly knock the brain off its typical course.

Developing the "Detached Observer"

In coaching we often talk about the concept of *detached observer*. The detached observer is a small witness on your shoulder. The detached observer is noticing things that are going on, but without great opinions or editorials about it. Self judgment is the person on your shoulder that not only sees what you do, but then makes you feel bad or criticizes you. The detached observer simply points out the behavior without the editorial, almost like the reality TV show cameraman. Many times I encourage the coachee to simply go out and watch themselves as a detached observer for the next week or two and come back and report what they noticed. It is only after observation that we begin to encourage them to see new choices and new paths they can create.

This concept and practice of a detached observer is the number one positive result coachees experience in coaching. The beauty of it is it tends to stay with you over a long period of time. Once you develop this muscle of detached observer it often stays with you for the rest of your life (even though at times you would love to fall back asleep!)

Take Your Time in the Analysis Step of the Coaching Process

One of the most common mistakes is not allowing enough time for the coachee to "marinate" in the analysis part of the coaching process. Remember, real transformation usually involves deeper thinking, more reflection, and choices. I know we are all in love with speed and efficiency, but now is not the time or place for speed in this part of the coaching process.

Great Coaches Ask Great Questions

So again, the temptation for most managers and leaders with "type A" personalities is to simply tell people what to do because, you and I both know, you have the best ideas! ☺ But great coaches ask great questions and help their coachees generate their own ideas, ideas that they will have the most ownership and commitment to. Most of this happens in Step two, the analysis phase of coaching.

Step 3: C for Commitment—"Pulling Us Up to New Heights"

We can see gaps. We can analyze our different options, but nothing changes until we make **commitments to new actions, attitudes, or behaviors**. Again, this is one of the most important pieces of the coaching process. Coachees have seen the gap, have come up with different choices for doing things differently, and now it is the coach's job to make sure that they make specific and actionable commitments to new behaviors. The commitment should be:

- Clear
- Measurable
- Timely
- Detailed

We are looking for new rituals, new behaviors and new actions.

One of the common mistakes is that a coach has been brave enough to unearth and work on the gap, has gotten the client to look at many new options, but then has "gone easy" on pushing the client to make a real, authentic and strong commitment.

Some examples of *specific* commitments might be:

- Have a conversation with someone by a certain day or time
- Make ten sales call a day
- Listen more
- Suspend judgment when someone is speaking
- Do a prioritized task list every morning before starting the day
- Call someone and apologize

Our figurine in the PACE™ process shows our coachee reaching for pitons (metal spikes used in rock climbing) in the mountain and pulling himself or herself up to new heights. This is a nice visual for what commitments are all about. One of the premises of how to reach higher levels of results is the concept of stretching yourself to new heights. Great coaches get *stretch commitments* out of their coachees. They empower, encourage, and engage the coachees to produce results that the coachees themselves are even surprised about.

Spiraling Up—The Road to Greatness

Hopefully, over time your coachees commit to generally continue going higher and higher. The only way to the top of the mountain is one crest at a time. So when you are thinking about the commitments that you are getting from your coachees, remember that it is a journey and a process.

Step 4: E for Execution—"The Finish Line"

What is all the coaching for if we do not produce a different result? We are now crossing the finish line. We saw a gap, analyzed our choices, made new commitments, and then we produced a new result. Did we? So, in this phase of the coaching process, we either:

- Agree upon what the outcome will look like; or
- Verify what the outcome actually was.

Again, because it is a recursive process, at this execution phase sometimes we will say, "Great, it's been done," and move on. Other times we will make adjustments based upon recent performance, and create further coaching commitments.

Follow-Up—Don't Forget to Be Waiting at the Finish Line!

One of the most common mistakes I see leaders make is that they did great work getting their teammates to stretch and go for a new result, yet they have no means of practice or *following up* and cheering at the finish line. Old leader (manager) behaviors show up and the leader spends all of his or her time and energy focusing on the next gap. One of the reasons coaching works is because the coach is acting as a *trusted supporter* and cheerleader in the coachee's journey. Remember, if the number one goal is to help team members become *self-generating and self-correcting*, you do need to encourage and celebrate success. It is an important step in the coaching process.

One Finish Line Becomes Another Starting Point

If the premise of this book is about coaching in business, and if your business is like most businesses, you never "arrive." So a few minutes after we finish the cheering at the finish line, great *coaching leaders* are asking the coachee, "What's next?" Every elite athlete, performer, and musician keeps breaking through and reaching new levels of performance. So when you become a great *coaching leader* and have a coaching culture, the "what's next" commitment follows naturally and effortlessly.

Let's Fill in More Detail Around the Process from the 5,000-Foot View

Okay, now that we've taken our first 5,000-foot view of the PACE™ coaching process, let's circle back and fill in some of the detail and surrounding landscape of the "how of coaching."

Obtain Permission to Coach

First and foremost, you should always have *permission to coach.* In an organizational setting, we assume that permission to coach is granted or implied in a direct supervisor and subordinate relationship. Many times, when you become a non-stop *coaching leader,* it is pretty much a given that those around you will be receiving coaching often. It may not be as obvious for every leader in every situation. The point is, you should continue to re-confirm permission to coach.

Earlier I talked about a leader who wanted to "switch gears" in a manager, direct report-type meeting. I encourage you, even in those types of settings, to "make room" for coaching by making an *explicit* request. Transparency is an important quality for building trust and rapport. I encourage you to use language like, "Could we have a *coaching conversation* about this?" or "Would you be open to some coaching on this?"

The "Dance" of the Coaching Conversation

By now you have a sense that coaching occurs in a coaching conversation. The typical coaching conversation may look a bit like a dance in a ballroom. One of my esteemed colleagues, David Rock, talks about the dance of the coaching conversation. As we are figuring out what the **perceived need** is, then we might get over into **analysis**, then we might work around in that for a while, and eventually get onto some firm ground called the new **commitments**. So, even though the PACE™ process appears to be very simple and straightforward, there is a real flow and artistry to the coaching conversation. Give yourself permission to be flexible and adaptive in the conversation.

The How of Coaching—Summary

To summarize what we learned so far about the how of coaching:

- Coaching happens mostly in *coaching conversations*.
- All coaching needs to start with a *perceived need*.
- To be effective, after *analysis* coaching must produce *new commitments to action*.
- You should always get *permission to coach* even if you think it is implied.

Before you go right out and start using the PACE™ coaching process, let's dive further into its details and help you become even more prepared.

COACH THE COACH

Look at the PACE™ coaching process and begin to reflect upon the perceived needs that you anticipate you would like to do some coaching on, either with your coachee or yourself. Go a step further and begin to think about the different kinds of analysis and awareness you might create relative to each of the perceived needs. Then go a step further and begin to anticipate what types of commitments would be made and how you could make sure those were specific and observable. Lastly, anticipate what the finish line might look like and the follow-up conversations based upon the perceived needs. Make some notes about that in anticipation of some coaching you will be doing in the future.

CHAPTER FOUR

P: Perceived Need

The Gap—The Place Where All Great Coaches Work

Here's the place where leaders, managers, and coaches all lose sleep at night. It is the difference between the current level of performance and the desired or potential level of performance.

Coaching leaders know that their coaching always starts with doing a good job of establishing the perceived need. Remember, this book is about creating real engagement, better execution, and better results. The key to real engagement is to have a clearly defined perceived need.

For many of you, this may seem obvious or simple given the fact that you are all business leaders. So in business, the perceived need is always to be more productive, effective, and make more money, right? The perceived need we are talking about here is the specific skill, attitude, and behavior that is needed from your team member to produce a higher level of result. The art of being a great *coaching leader* is about how the perceived need gets established.

Concrete and Specific is the Key

The more specific you can be in the determination of the perceived need, the more successful you are going to be in coaching. Different types of perceived needs lend themselves to more specificity. Any time you can be more specific, it is better.

Seen and Unseen

Many perceived needs present themselves obviously in terms of breakdowns or missed performance mileposts. Other perceived needs may be less noticeable to your team members. You might see a team member struggling in some form and that may be the moment to ask them if they would be open to coaching.

"Why is This Important?" is a Critical Question

We want to establish the gap, or the perceived need, but at the same time the "why is it important?" question helps anchor the perceived need. When someone can see how this gap in their performance is impacting them on a bigger picture and more strategic level, it helps them stay focused on and motivated to work on the gap. Great *coaching leaders* always make finding out about the "why it is important," a routine in the perceived need step of the coaching conversation.

Layers Upon Layers—a Recursive Process

You will quickly see in coaching that it is a little bit like what we call "peeling back the onion." Most perceived needs can be connected to other perceived needs and on and on. Remember, coaching is a recursive process so we fully expect the perceived needs to continue to go deeper or become more complex as the relationship progresses.

One of the best signs that you are progressing as a *coaching leader* is that the level of the coaching conversations and the outcomes you are working toward become even more meaningful and rewarding. You know you are becoming a great *coaching leader* when you see not only the level of your coaching going up, but the level of results and the quality of people you are attracting going up as well.

Who is Responsible for Determining the Perceived Need?

You are ultimately responsible as the *coaching leader* to make sure that the gaps or perceived needs are always clearly articulated. Your goal is to have your team members continually look to uncover and declare their own perceived needs. We know people are more motivated when they have ownership or authorship. It is your responsibility, but in the end, it would be great if the coachee was coming up with their own perceived needs.

LET'S "LISTEN IN"

John is the CEO at a medium-sized construction firm in Texas. One of his project managers, Mary, seems to consistently miss deadlines on deliverables to the team members.

John: "I didn't receive your job cost report on Friday for the Camelback Road job."

Mary: "Yeah, I got slammed late last week on the Indian School Road job and didn't have time to get the Camelback job cost report in."

John: "I know we've talked before about the importance of meeting our commitments with each other relative to project reports. What happened?"

Mary: "My crew foreman, Joe, called me and said he wanted me to come out and look at that drainage issue on the Indian School job."

John: "I can appreciate the fact that you get pulled in so many different directions, but hopefully you can appreciate the fact that I've been tasked with presenting all of our job cost updates to Ron every

Tuesday. Without your report on Friday, I'm unable to prepare and be ready to do my job on Tuesday."

Mary: "I understand. I'm sorry I let you down."

John: "Would you be open to a coaching conversation about this?"

Mary: "Sure."

John: "So what do you think is the gap here, Mary? What's missing? What is the real issue?"

Mary: "I guess I ultimately need to learn how to prioritize my work."

John: "Great, I'm glad that you see that. What's it going to cost you if you don't learn how to prioritize your work?

Mary: "Probably my job, or more importantly, my career as a project manager."

John: "That sounds right. I want to acknowledge you for seeing the bigger picture. So what do you think you need to do to become better at prioritizing?"

So can you see that as a coach, John could have invited Mary into the coaching conversation and allowed her to say that the perceived need was learning how to get her job cost report done every Friday? At the same time, by taking a moment or two longer, John was able to uncover the bigger, more strategic issue of her inability to prioritize work.

Did you also see that John made an effort to further "cement in" the perceived need by helping Mary understand or state the bigger picture (potentially losing her job or career)?

LET'S LISTEN IN AGAIN:

John: "So it sounds like you realize you need to learn how to prioritize your work—that's good. I'm trying to become the most effective coach I can be, so I want to make sure that we get very clear about the gap that we're working on. Can you be more specific about what you mean by prioritizing your work?"

Mary: "I guess I mean being able to prioritize it so that I can get it done in the time frame allotted."

John: "How would we know if you are successful at that?" *(another great coaching question)*

Mary: "My work would be done on time and I would meet the commitments I had made to others."

John: "Good. So what we're working on is you being able to prioritize your work, get it done on time, and meet your commitment to others. Why don't we start to look at how we can close that gap?"

So you can see that by taking a few more minutes and asking a few more questions, John was able to further solidify and get specific about the perceived need. These extra steps are going to make the next few steps in coaching even more effective.

What If I Can't Get the Coachee to Come Up With the Perceived Need?

In the beginning of your coaching endeavors, it is not uncommon for you or the coachee to fumble around a bit as you come up with the perceived need. That's okay, do not let it deter you.

Becoming fluent in the coaching conversation takes practice and patience. I will ask you to trust the coaching process and believe me when I say, in the end, coaching is going to provide you great satisfaction and relief as a leader. So when starting, be patient; give yourself and the coachee time to learn the process and flow of the coaching conversation.

On the other hand, if you have a coachee who simply refuses to cooperate or generate perceived needs, you may have identified a team member who was not going to fit into the coaching culture. That's okay too. I have always said that coaching is an *accelerator*. One of the ways that coaching can accelerate the process is your identification of people that are willing and able to be open to coaching and developing new skills. So, if someone cannot buy into the coaching idea and is very reluctant about coming up with perceived needs, I suggest you invite them to self-select off the team.

We Are Always Training Others How to Treat Us

This is one of my favorite concepts. If you think about it, we are all teaching each other how we would like to interact with each other, even if it is almost subconscious on one level. As a *coaching leader* it will be imperative that you are consistent, determined, and unrelenting about having people being open to coaching. Remember, they have a choice about working with any leader they choose (even though most people forget this or don't acknowledge it) so if they do not like it—take a hike!

The concept of "training others" can be illuminating in all relationships in your life. I had a co-worker many years ago who, every time I tried to give her feedback, would immediately become emotional, combative, and defensive. So if we think about it, she is in a way trying to send me the message, "If you give me feedback, I'm going to blow up." Most people would become "trained" into not giving feedback, and trust me, I was tempted to accept that training. Instead, I would let her blow up, and then I would calmly and methodically go ahead and give her my feedback. Eventually she stopped blowing up because she realized that I had in fact "trained her" that I was going to continue to give feedback regardless of her outbursts. In most cases, people stop those types of behaviors when they realize they are not going to get their desired outcome.

As a *coaching leader always train them* about what it's going to take to be on your team!

Step One: Perceived Need Summary
- Always be as specific as you can be.
- Do not forget the "why is this important?" question.
- Remember the perceived needs will get deeper and more complex if you are doing your job right.
- Train people that they need to learn how to come up with perceived needs.

COACH THE COACH

What are your performance gaps right now as a leader?

What is important about closing those gaps?

Have you come up with the most concrete detail of the gap?

Take fifteen minutes and run through your own self-coaching conversation and practice on yourself to uncover and articulate your gaps. We will use those as we move through the next steps in the following chapters.

CHAPTER FIVE

A: Analysis—The Choices We Have in Front of Us

Okay, I know you are excited, you got the coachee to see their perceived need and now comes the easy part, just tell them what to do to close the gap. Wrong! That is what managers or old school leaders do and that is the reason those styles of leadership rarely create true buy-in and/or motivation to change.

Coaching leaders know that the real bedrock of coaching is **choice.** In this step of the PACE™ coaching process we are not actually going to create choice, yet; first we want the coachee to see *what is really going on* and the *wide array of possible choices* they have before they actually choose (Step Three—commitments to action).

In this step in the coaching process there is tremendous value in getting people to slow down and take a careful look at what is really going on in regard to their performance.

Detached Observer

I often ask people to pretend they have a reality TV show film crew following them around to give us a documentary-type view of what is going on in their world. The idea here is that we want to see their actions, reactions, and emotions without the commentary—their justifications and "stories" about why they are doing what they are doing. I call this learning how to be a "detached observer." In most cases, clients cite it as one of the most meaningful and powerful outcomes of the coaching process. When you can learn how to separate yourself from yourself and be a detached observer, it gives you powerful access to seeing new courses of action in your life.

The brain scientists tell us that the brain is always trying to hardwire routine behaviors so it can save its resources to figure out new things. This explains why so many of our routine behaviors and actions occur on *autopilot*. The ***coaching leader's*** role is to get the coachee to turn off the *autopilot* and start to take back control of their thinking, actions, and results.

Stop and Take Inventory Before Anything Else

So in Step Two the coach's role is to help the coachee begin to take inventory about what is really happening in regard to their performance. That inventory process could take a variety of courses. Remember, because coaching is a recursive process, the inventory may take place over a period of a few coaching sessions. Many times when coachees talk about a perceived need at the end of this part of the conversation, I might send them out to be a detached observer and watch what is really going on during the action of their performance.

Another way to take inventory is to simply reflect in the coaching session and recall what they think is going on in regard to performance. The coach acts as a sounding board as the coachee recalls what is going on.

The Power of Reflection

The magic happens when people begin to be thoughtful and reflective about what they are doing. This is the magic that is available in Step Two of the PACE™ coaching process. When we stop and reflect, somehow it allows us to have broader and diverse perspectives about how our thoughts fit into the bigger picture.

Many times reflection brings a *quieter mind* and in turn more creativity to solve complex problems. Reflection also allows us to remove ourselves a bit from the situation and be more detached and *objective*. Reflection also provides the coach much more information about the coachee's thinking. As the coachee shares their reflections with the coach, it is almost like turning on the TV, but this time in high definition, so we see much more that will allow us to ask better questions and the coachee can see new things about themselves.

In addition, written reflection can help us capture and preserve meaningful insights in our life journey. As I was recently planning for another year in my coaching business, I took out and reviewed some written reflections from the prior year and got reconnected to some great insights I had captured in my journal. As a coach you like to make an impact in the present day, but imagine how great it would be to give the coachee practices, like reflective journaling, that could provide insights for many years to come.

Rewinding the "Game Tape"

Another common technique or terminology we use in coaching is the idea of rewinding the "game tape." When you think about elite athletes, great musicians or even physicians, you know that they benefit from reviewing their performances after the fact.

In the analysis step of the PACE™ coaching process, it is very common for us to have the client recount the performance and situation that they are working on. Rewinding the game tape is used in this step as well as in the fourth step coming up. It may often be difficult to make adjustments and understand what is going on in real time for many people; this is why giving them the time and space to replay their performance can be helpful to them.

As a ***coaching leader,*** you might ask the coachee to rewind some game tape or you may be the one to replay the game tape. Either way, it allows you both to be in the mindset of the commentator up in the booth taking an objective view of the performance and looking for ways to improve.

Don't Forget—Don't "Buy" Their Story

As a coach, one of the most common traps is to "buy into" the coachee's story without challenging their *narrative.* When I use the term "narrative," I am referring to the idea that we are all "linguistic beings," that words are "the water that we swim in." Like the fish in the ocean, we are oblivious to the fact that we are in the water because we have been in the water our whole life. A personal narrative is the story they are creating about themselves, but it is a story filled with a lot of interpretation, editorial opinions, and personal biases. Somewhere in there are a certain number of facts, but for the most part it is 50% fact and 50% storytelling.

Let me call upon my teacher, Julio Olalla, who says in coaching we get to "break the transparency" of their story. Think of your editorial opinions as the windshield you are looking through in your car. You forget that it is even there until it gets a crack and then you realize you have been looking through it. That is what Julio is referring to. As coaches we want to get people to see their filters and interpretations.

Your role as their coach is to challenge everything about the story. This is how you help the coachee break out of their myopic, hardwired brain into new creative ways of solving their problems. If you, as their coach, simply buy into their story, you will not be able to stay objective, ask good questions, or help them create a more personally powerful or inspiring story.

I want you to be a compassionate listener. I encourage you to be a bit generous and patient in allowing of them to tell their story; just don't become a character in the story! In fact, as you let them meander in their story, oftentimes you may begin to see patterns of their thinking or the revealing of their values and most foundational narratives.

You begin to see themes in people's thinking and worldview. As a coach, this allows you to point those patterns out to the coachee and get them to start to challenge whether those patterns of thinking are serving them well. Oftentimes, coachees have limiting beliefs, invalid stories, or are using old strategies that are no longer serving them. All of these are opportunities for the coach to challenge the coachee.

Friend vs. Coach—a Fine Line

Here is a critical moment in the *art of coaching*. Learning how to be a compassionate, generous listener and caring partner and still be able to call them on their story. The more you can learn how to master this move in coaching, the sooner you will become a masterful coach.

Beware of Your Story and Narratives

Another potential pitfall is for you to allow your own story, biases, and narratives to impact how you are listening to the story. In this phase of the coaching process, it is critically important to be a detached observer and ask questions with an open and unbiased mind. As a coach, if you allow your biases to impact your questions, it could send the conversation off on the wrong course. Great coaches develop the ability to bear witness, ask questions, and challenge people without bringing their own dramas and stories into the equation.

The Two Sides to Awareness—What's Going On and What Are Our Choices?

The first side of awareness is about having the coachee accurately assess what is going on relative to their performance. This is where detached observer, reflection, and performance journaling may be required. This could occur over several performances over several weeks so that the coachee gets to see a broader view of the performance and the ability to see bigger patterns.

The second side of awareness is about assessing the variety of choices for new thinking, new action, and new skills that are available. Oftentimes the coach and the coachee get so excited about the fact that they have identified a perceived need, and have done a nice job of observing what is going on in the performance, that they tend to quickly make a decision about what to do differently. Avoid the trap of allowing the coachee to go with their first choice.

You have come this far; make sure to take your time and explore the *wide variety* of choices that are available for taking new action. You may want to encourage the coachee to try several of their options over a period of time as a way to determine their best course of action.

Stirring Up Creativity and Resourcefulness

Such an important part of Step Two is helping people tap into their creativity and resourcefulness. The hardwired myopic brain stifles a huge amount of creativity that is available to the coachee. As a coach, your job in the process is to create the space, time, and good questions to allow the coachee to see all of the choices that are available. This is a huge gift to the coachee and very important in terms of helping them generate new ways of thinking and taking action.

"Trying On" Different Choices

In this phase of the coaching, it is really important to allow the coachee to "try on" different ways of looking at the situation and different ways of taking new action. I will literally say to the client, "Why don't you try that on for a moment and see how it feels," a new perspective, a new potential way of taking action. This is a hugely important part of coaching. In real life, in real time, we do not have the option of trying on different perspectives and different types of action. To allow that in coaching is a really important part of the process.

New Perspectives

One of the most common outcomes of coaching is to empower people to see new perspectives about how they are approaching their challenges or opportunities. Remember, the myopic, hardwired brain takes away so many of those new perspectives. The ability to generate new perspectives is a critically important skill for staying creative in solving complex problems.

People get invested in their perspectives. They get invested in being right or having their story be the one and only true story. As a coach, it is important to challenge, cajole and even knock them off the perch of their fixed perspective. Helping people create a new story about their life is one of the most rewarding aspects of coaching.

Deep Listening

Coaching leaders are listening in a very deep way. They are listening for strongly *embedded patterns of thinking*, old stories and blind spots. They are listening for emotion, body language, dreams, and desires as well as nonverbal cues that are indicators of where the coachee may be undermining their success.

There is Wisdom in the Silence

Sometimes in coaching, we talk about listening for what is *not* being said. As coaches, many times we get uncomfortable or impatient for action when silence is occurring. Many times this is where the greatest breakthroughs are about to happen. Be patient and let the client sit in silence and generate their own breakthroughs.

When we were working with an executive team many years ago in a group coaching setting, the group was talking about all of the issues that were impeding their progress or contributing to the gap we were working on. I had asked, "Is there anything else?" And there was about thirty seconds of silence. I was getting impatient and ready to move on and my fellow coach, Donna, was listening for what was not being said and sensed there was something there. She gave me a subtle hand signal which said, "Don't move, just sit for another minute." She then said something like, "Are you sure there is nothing else, because I feel like there is something more you want to say?" and sure enough, out it came. They said, "Yeah, it seems like Kim (their manager) does not trust us," and there it was, the elephant in the room, the "aha moment," the most important thing for us to work on with this group.

Do not be afraid of the silence.

Seems Like a Lot, But Eventually Could Happen in Just a Few Moments

As you listen to all of the steps, possible courses of action, and things to be thinking about in coaching, I can imagine it may seem a little overwhelming. As you become more *fluent in the coaching conversation,* all of these steps can happen in a very short period of time and without you having to think about all of this. It is important for you to have a sense of the whole "lay of the land," but I can assure you that it all unfolds more quickly and effortlessly as you become masterful.

Let's revisit the coaching conversation with John and Mary to see what Step Two sounds like in action.

LISTEN IN—JOHN AND MARY STEP TWO ANALYSIS

John: "So Mary, can we continue helping you close the gap on being able to prioritize your work and meet your commitments?"

Mary: "Yeah, sure."

John: "Thanks for being open to the coaching. As you think about not prioritizing and not meeting your commitments, what do you think gets in your way?

Mary: "As I said before, I seem to get overwhelmed with work and lose track of the priorities and commitments."

John: "Do you see any pattern about when and how this occurs? Does it happen at the end of the day or the end of the week or just any time?"

Mary: "I usually start the week off with a sense of what I need to do and what the priorities are, but as the week unfolds I tend to lose the handle on it."

John: "Why do you think it happens that way?"

Mary: "I think that with all of the best intentions the reality of the day and week unfolds and I end up having to deal with a lot of unexpected emergencies and get off track."

John: "I must admit that does sound like our industry (demonstrating empathy—yet doesn't fully buy into the story) but I know we need to figure out a way around this. If you think you watched yourself like we were doing a reality TV show about you, what would we see in terms of your energy, focus, and emotions as you go through your day?"

Mary: "I think you would see me pretty rested, focused, calm, and ready to go at the beginning of the week and at the beginning of the day, but as the days wear on, I tend to get a little tired, overwhelmed, and yes, a bit emotional as break-downs occur and things don't turn out the way we planned."

John: "Let me ask you another question. Do you take any breaks, eat lunch, or stop and catch your breath during the day?"

Mary: "No. You know our life—it's go, go, go from the minute we wake up."

John: "Do you think there would be any value in trying to stop and take a break and give your body a little bit of fuel during the day?"

Mary: "I guess it probably would help, but I feel like if I stopped I would be more overwhelmed." (limiting belief)

John: "I can see why you think that; it almost makes sense. But at the same time I am wondering if you stopped and re-fueled if it wouldn't give you more effective energy. I am thinking a little bit about the race car drivers and how they have to stop for a pit stop even in the middle of a difficult race. Do you think you'd be willing to give it a try?"

Mary: "Yeah, I guess I could try it."

John: "I have an idea. How about if over this next week you simply "watch yourself" in action and give yourself permission to take a break a couple of times throughout the day, and in that break you not only take a breather, eat a little something, but also reflect upon what you noticed about how you are working. Would you be willing to do that?"

Mary: "Yeah, I would be willing to try it. I really want to get better at what I do."

John: "Great. Don't try to do too much. This first week I want you to give yourself permission to just notice more; don't try to solve the problem. Does that make sense? I think we should first get a better handle on what is going on before we try to come up with some ideas for how we solve it? Okay?"

Mary: "Okay, I will try it."

We can see how John has tried to help Mary begin to focus on awareness in regard to her performance tendencies. They have begun to identify some new action, but not too much. The majority of the focus is about awareness of what is going on, not awareness about new choices or new actions. Let's go back a week later and listen in.

John: "So how did it go last week? What did you notice?"

Mary: "I must admit it was pretty interesting during the whole "detached observer" thing."

John: "It usually is! What did you notice about Mary?"

Mary: "Just as I suspected, I was doing pretty well most of the day on Monday, until mid-afternoon when the Tatum project got derailed."

John: "What did you notice when things went off track?"

Mary: "I noticed that when my job foreman Bruce dropped the ball for the fiftieth time, I got so angry

I almost lost it! After that, the rest of the day was a bit of a blur."

John: "Good job noticing and good job not losing it completely! So what did you learn from that?"

Mary: "I learned that my job is a lot harder because Bruce is an idiot."

John: "Maybe. But when you notice this in regard to your patterns, prioritization, and commitments, what did you see? (Refocuses the client on the perceived need.)

Mary: "I noticed that when I get very angry my focus and process get derailed."

John: "That is an important thing to notice—good job. (Now switches from awareness of what is happening to awareness of new choices). What do you think you could do different next week?"

Mary: "Get Bruce fired. I have been saying for a long time he is a liability."

John: "That is one choice." (Lets Mary vent a bit but doesn't buy in to the story) "Do you see any other choices?"

Mary: "I guess first and foremost I should figure out how to not get so upset when somebody drops the ball."

John: "Good thinking. What else?"

Mary: "I guess I could think of a way to get Bruce to do his job."

John: "What else?" (Keeps the client generating more awareness of choices.)

Mary: "I guess I should figure out a way to keep my priorities and commitments in focus even in the midst of breakdowns."

John: "Exactly—great!"

So we can see that John allowed Mary two weeks to spend time getting awareness about what was really going on and then began to help her uncover some awareness about new actions she could take.

Did you notice that even though John agrees with Mary that something should be done about Bruce, he did not allow the coaching to get off track and go down that road. He stayed focused on helping Mary generate good awareness about what was going on and what her choices were. He helped Mary work on Mary. Oftentimes coachees will try to work on other people in their coaching session. Don't allow them to do that!

More Roads to Go Down for Future Conversations

If I were Mary's coach, I would be making mental notes of other roads we could travel in future coaching conversations. Why does Mary get so upset? Has this been a pattern of hers for many years? Is there another reason why Bruce causes her more upset than other people? Where else does she allow her emotions to get the best of her and allow her performance to drop? Why doesn't she take better care of herself?

There are lots of roads to go down with the coachee over the course of many coaching conversations.

Step Two: Analysis Summary

Step Two of the PACE™ coaching process is all about analysis of information and choices. Many times the coaching *process* enables the coachee to simply stop and be reflective. While there are an unlimited number of options for analysis, my experience is that the most common areas of analysis are:

- What are the *facts* about the performance gap?
- What *patterns* (thinking, acting, mindset) are present?
- What are the various *choices* of new actions and patterns to create?

Great coaches ask great questions! They are patient and allow people to see things in a new light. Be patient in Step Two because the ability to see all of the choices will greatly impact the quality of Step Three in the types of commitments the coachee makes.

COACH THE COACH

Knowing what you know about yourself, reflect upon how you think you'll handle the Analysis step in the PACE™ coaching process.

- Are you generally patient in allowing people to come up with new ways of approaching things, or are you the type that finds yourself giving them the answers?
- Do you think you can ask questions and allow them to generate their own ideas?
- Can you refrain from bringing your own judgments and interpretations as they generate their own thinking?

Based upon your reflections, what are one to three new practices you should begin in order to be an effective *coaching leader?*

CHAPTER SIX

C: Commitment—Where the Rubber Meets the Road

The stage is set. We did a great job of uncovering the perceived need, and helped them to see many new perspectives and choices. Now is the time to turn all of that good work into commitments!

Commitments—Where the Rubber Meets the Road

It is one thing to *talk* about new perspectives and new actions; it is another to commit to it and take action. This is my favorite step in the PACE™ coaching process. People theorize and intellectualize about what they should do differently, but none of that means anything unless they commit to new actions, new thinking and new behaviors.

What We Mean by Commitment

A commitment is *a promise to act or think a certain way.* There is a whole other book that I could write on commitment. One of my favorite teachers, Robert Keegan, says that he does not care about what people say, he only cares about what they are committed to. We can see what they are committed to by their actions. I have always been intrigued by this observation.

I want to say to people, "What I want to know most about you is what you are *committed* to?"

Step Three: Making Measurable Commitments

Let's go back to the coaching conversation. You have clearly identified the perceived need. You have taken time to build awareness about not only patterns of thinking and action but also potential new choices for action. Now it is time for the coach to invite the coachee to make commitments based upon the first two steps of the process.

Specific, Clear, and Measurable

It sounds obvious, but many times new *coaching leaders* get so excited about the fact that they have uncovered the perceived need and got the coachee to generate new choices that they allow the coachee to leave the coaching conversation with *weak* or *unclear* commitments. Take your time and get good at making sure the coachee makes specific, clear, and measurable commitments.

Sometimes specific, clear, and measurable is best uncovered through the measurement of *observable*. In other words if we cannot see it, touch it, or feel it, then it is probably not a very good commitment.

Realistic and Reasonable

Do not forget as a *coaching leader* it is part of your job to make sure the coachee is committed to *realistic* and *reasonable* courses of action. We all want big dramatic breakthrough levels of performance, but you are not doing the coachee or yourself any good by allowing people to leave the coaching session with unrealistic or overly ambitious commitments.

This is a fine line to walk. You want to see the coachee stretching and challenging themselves to reach new heights of performance. So, you need to be careful to help them find that delicate line between a stretch goal and an unrealistic goal.

Building Confidence in the Process

One of the things you are always trying to protect is confidence in the coaching process. If you allow people to make unrealistic commitments and they come up short, their confidence in you and the coaching process will be undermined. Confidence is such a delicate and powerful thing in coaching and performance.

Strive to invite the coachee to make commitments that will build skill and stretch their capacity, but at the same time build their sense of accomplishment and confidence in their own ability. If they lose confidence in themselves, their coach, or the coaching process, it can be nearly impossible to get it back.

Types of Commitments—Awareness—Attitude—Action

When we are talking about commitments, it is easy to think that we are always talking about *action*, but we may not be. Many times I am inviting a client to commit to looking for new perspectives, attitudes, and mindsets as a precursor for later commitment for new action.

Even when we get that commitment to new attitudes or new perspectives, it is important to be *specific* and to hold them accountable to that.

Commitments That Lead to More Commitments

Again, do not forget about the recursive nature of coaching. The commitments they make this week in coaching most likely will lead to bigger and deeper commitments in subsequent weeks of coaching. You are really trying to help the client get acclimated to the coaching process and learn how to make and keep good commitments. As the coachee learns how to be a good coachee, it becomes easier and more effortless to generate new, meaningful, and powerful commitments.

Strong Language Equals Strong Commitments

Humans are linguistic beings; *words are the water that we swim in.* As a *coaching leader* it is imperative that you are *meticulous* and *rigorous* about the word choices in the commitments being made.

Consider this: Coachee says, "Yeah, I'll try to keep an eye out for when I get distracted and off-track in my work," versus "I will pay close attention to my work habits next week and identify times when I get off track." Can you see how the first statement inherently gives the coachee permission to come back and say it did not happen? Do not allow commitments to be made with weak, wishy-washy language!

LET'S LISTEN IN AGAIN TO JOHN COACHING MARY AND SEE HOW THE COMMITMENTS UNFOLD:

John: "So you have agreed that you need to find a way to keep your emotional balance, even when breakdowns occur. What do you think you need to do to make that happen?"

Mary: "I guess I should come up with some way of taking a quick break right after an upset occurs to try to give myself enough time to cool off a bit."

John: "That sounds like a good idea. Can you be more specific about exactly what that will look like?"

Mary: "When a breakdown or anything occurs and I notice an emotional reaction, I will give myself permission to take a couple of moments to breathe and calm down."

John: "Good. That sounds observable. So next time we are together I am going to ask you to give me some examples of times where you able to do that, okay?"

Mary: "Okay."

John: "The other thing we identified was that you wanted to be able to stay focused and on track with your priorities even when things get hectic. What do you think you need to commit to so you can make that happen?"

Mary: "I have a task list on my computer but when I get overwhelmed I don't look at it."

John: "I'm glad you see that. Remember awareness is a new result we are going for, so I'm glad you are noticing that. What else do you need to commit to now that you know that?"

Mary: "I guess I should try to remember to review my computer task list even when I am overwhelmed."

John: "It seems like we are headed in the right direction, but if you don't mind me saying, when I hear things like "should" and "try" it makes me nervous about the true level of the commitment. It seems like you are committed to doing this. Can you think of any other way that you could language this or say this in a way that would be even stronger?

Mary: "Why don't I say, I will review my computer task list even when I'm overwhelmed."

John: "Much better, that's stronger. But it made me think of something else. If your task list is an important part of staying on track and keeping your commitments, would it make sense that you review it at a certain time of day, every day, regardless of what's going on or how overwhelmed you are?"

Mary: "Good point. I do intend to look at it throughout the day but as I say, when I get overwhelmed that seems to go away."

John: "Are you willing to commit to a certain number of times or a certain time of day that you would review your task list?

Mary: "Great idea. Why don't I say that my commitment is that I will review my task list after lunch and at the end of the day regardless of the success/stress/workload of the day?"

John: "That sounds really solid. So when we get together again next week, I will be asking you to be accountable for how many days you were able to keep this commitment. Remember this is all about you being the best project manager you can be and having a successful career."

Mary: "Yeah, I got it. Thanks for helping me work through this and come up with the commitment."

Commitments Driving the Stake Deep into the Ground

You can see that John could have accepted the first version of the commitment, which was to look at her task list even if she got overwhelmed, but John, being the great *coaching leader* that he is, continued to work with Mary and the result was an even more powerful commitment to look at the task list every day, regardless of the day's activities. That makes the commitment even clearer and deeper because it is going to happen every day.

Commitments in Context and "Nested" Commitments

The other thing John did was to place the commitment in the context of the bigger commitment—being a great project manager and having a successful career. Sometimes we refer to this as "nested" commitments. The daily commitment ties into the bigger commitment of being a successful project manager, which ties into the bigger commitment of having a successful career, which ties into the bigger commitment of making a good living and reaching retirement with a healthy savings account.

Great *coaching leaders* are always reminding their team about how all of those commitments go together to form the bigger vision.

Step Three: Commitment Summary
- Make sure the commitments are clear and observable
- Look for opportunities for the commitments to be driven in deeper
- Keep the commitments in context of other commitments
- Often ask for several commitments on each perceived need

COACH THE COACH

Rewind the "game tape" and review your own ability to solicit commitments from your team members.

- Is it one of your leadership strengths or opportunities for improvement?
- Are the commitments you receive clear, measurable, and strong?
- Do you drive the commitments deeper by connecting them with people's bigger picture vision?

- Can you see how nested commitments are in play?
- What are the one to three actions you can take to have your team generate even more effective commitments?

CHAPTER SEVEN

E: Execution—The Finish Line and Starting Gate

This is the reason we coach: to produce the desired results; to reach our potential; to achieve high business goals; and to increase profits and personal satisfaction.

Levels of Success

In coaching, as in business, sometimes good progress is, in itself, success. To say it another way, if the coachee comes back and has made progress toward the new skills and behaviors, that is a win. If they have achieved all that they wanted to achieve in this particular outcome, many times that is the opening for the *coaching leader* to stretch the team member and create even higher levels of goals and results. That is part of the beauty of the coaching process and coaching style of leadership!

An Important Part of the Process

This fourth step is a bit like reaching the finish line in a race. It is a marker in time and represents an accomplishment. When I think about business and the *coaching leader,* I think about a marathon. If you are to enjoy long-term success in business, you need to keep running and creating new finish lines. Your competitors will force you to keep inventing new and higher levels of performance. That is the very nature of the free market system.

This step is important to build confidence in the coachee involved in the *coaching process*. Every time there is a successful outcome (or even progress toward outcomes) it gives the coachee a sense of accomplishment and creates motivation to keep working toward even higher levels of results.

Time for Celebration and Acknowledgment

One important role of the *coaching leader* is to be a bit of a cheerleader on the sidelines. Think about the Olympic athlete, who after so much training and hard work, reaches the ultimate level of success—the gold-medal. The coach is always close by with congratulations and acknowledgement of the hard work. At that moment, the coach-coachee relationship enjoys a moment of mutual success. When we think again about the Olympic athlete, the athlete is getting the majority of the recognition and they are certainly the one given the gold medal. In business, when your teammates succeed, you succeed by having more talented, effective, loyal, and productive employees. In that way the *coaching leaders* have an even better job than the Olympic coach!

An Important Place for Follow-up

One of the most common pitfalls of business leaders is their inability to follow up in a *consistent* and *methodical* manner. The E in the PACE™ coaching process *builds in* the follow-up. In fact, if you remember when we listened in during Step Three, John was already preparing Mary for the follow-up conversation when he said, "When we get together again I will be expecting you to report on how you have been reviewing your task list." Great *coaching leaders* are always weaving that dialogue about the finish line into the coaching conversation.

Reviewing the "Game Tape": an Opportunity for More Coaching

More often than not, after the performance, *coaching leaders* are working with the coachees to see how they can improve upon their technique and build even higher levels of performance. Celebrate what you accomplished, but at the same time begin the next coaching conversation enroute to the next accomplishment. It is a fine line to walk and one that great *coaching leaders* know how to orchestrate.

Another potential outcome is that little or no result was accomplished. In these cases, each party usually has an opportunity to look back and see if the perceived need was clearly articulated, whether there was true motivation, or whether the best course of action was chosen in the commitment stage. In all of those scenarios it is an opportunity for both the coach and the coachee to learn and improve for the future.

Critique for the Coach

Coaching leaders accept responsibility for the outcome. They are always questioning themselves in terms of their technique, and how they assessed the best course of action in coaching the coachee. Many times, the finish line is a nice time for the coach to reevaluate his or her effectiveness and/or reconsider how they have approached coaching with this particular team member.

LET'S GO BACK AND LISTEN IN TO THE FOURTH STEP WITH JOHN AND MARY:

John: "So how did your week go? How did you do in regard to the commitments you made in last week's coaching session?

Mary: "I did a much better job keeping an eye on my task list this week."

John: "That's good news! Congratulations! I know we are always trying to go for specific and measurable results. You committed to reviewing your task list twice every afternoon, so over the five-day period how many times would you say you reviewed it? (Notice John both acknowledged the success but is pushing as a *coaching leader* to hold Mary accountable to specific results in yet another artful way.)

Mary: "I think I did it twice on three days and once on two days. So I guess that would be eight out of ten times."

John: "That sounds like a pretty high level of result. Are you satisfied with that level of result?" (John testing Mary's resolve about her own personal greatness.)

Mary: "It is definitely a huge improvement, but I think if I am going to be as good as I want to be, I need to check it ten out of ten times."

John: "I am glad you said that because I was thinking the same thing. Not checking it a couple of times can create the opportunity for you to have breakdowns."

John: "So what is your commitment in regard to the task list for next week?"

Mary: "Ten out of ten!"

John: "Is there anything else you will need to do to achieve it ten out of ten times?"

Mary: "Continue to stay focused and committed to playing at the highest level."

John: "Okay. Anything else you want to report from this week?

Mary: "Not that I can think of. I am really pleased about the increased focus on my task list."

John: "Do you remember the commitment to stay emotionally calm if breakdowns occur?"

Mary: "Oh, yeah."

John: "So what did you notice with that commitment this week?

Mary: "I actually was able to do well with that when a breakdown occurred Tuesday morning. I consciously took a minute or two to catch my breath before I began to dive in and solve the problem. I wasn't as good on Thursday when another breakdown occurred and I lost my cool with the project foreman."

John: "Good work on Tuesday. What went wrong on Thursday?"

Mary: "That project has been extra frustrating because I do not have a great relationship with the client. I think that contributed to my anger."

John: "Good noticing. What do you think you could do different in the future?"

Mary: "Perhaps on a project like that, I need to put myself on extra careful awareness, knowing that there is that underlying high level of frustration to begin with."

John: "Good thinking. Are there any other projects right now that fall into that category?"

Mary: "Yeah, the State Route 51 project is with the same client."

John: "Okay so you are going to put yourself on extra awareness on that project?"

Mary: "Yes."

John: "Is there anything else we should discuss that you would like to commit to before our next coaching meeting?"

Mary: "No, I am good for now. Thanks for the support; it really felt good to have a more success-ful week this week."

John: "Thank you for being open to coaching, reaching a higher level of result, and keeping your commitments. You know that is going to help all of us be more successful. See you next week."

You can see that many things happened in this Fourth Step. There was some celebrating of success, but there was also some additional coaching going on when John said, "What went wrong on Thursday?" At that moment, there was a whole other PACE™ occurring about Thursday. There was more awareness when John asked, "Are there any other projects that fall into that category?"

You see so many elements of the PACE™ coaching process occurring again and again, in layer upon layer, in the coaching conversations. I know it may seem a little overwhelming at first, or almost confusing, but the more you become comfortable with the PACE™ process, the more you can manage multiple coach-ing conversations within bigger conversations. Trust me, you will get there!

Step Four—Execution Summary

The E step of the PACE™ coaching process is important for a number of reasons:

- For follow-up in the coaching process
- For building confidence in the coachee and the coaching process
- To celebrate the successes
- To identify new coaching opportunities
- For the coach to do some self-evaluation

COACH THE COACH

Review the "game tape" and see how well you do as a *coaching leader* at:

- Standing at the "finish line" and celebrating the success of your team members
- Following up on commitments made by your team to improve
- Encouraging people to set a new performance goal after they accomplished one

Identify one to three new practices you can implement to become a more effective *coaching leader.*

CHAPTER EIGHT

Start and Keep Coaching

Ready, Set, Go!

Until now, I talked about why you should coach. You have been prepared to become a coach. You have been given a coaching process and now what happens? Nothing. Truthfully, too many times leaders know they need to coach, they understand it is the right thing to do, but they are very reluctant to go out and coach.

The reluctance is because most leaders are highly successful, confident people with many years of experience. Who wants to go out and look bad in front of their team? Nobody!

If you bring the twenty qualities of a *coaching leader,* plus a little common sense and a willingness to learn, you are not only going to be fine, you are going to be surprised with the results you and your coachees will produce in a short amount of time.

Coach Early and Coach Often!

There are many ways and places to coach, but I want you to err on the side of *over-coaching,* not under-coaching. *Repetition* is the key to success. Every time you coach, you are building your coaching repertoire and muscle. Every time you let coaching slip by, you are sending the wrong message to your team that it is not important. Coaching happens in thousands of conversations over the course of a career. The greatest coaches are coaching almost all the time. There are probably a hundred opportunities to coach in any given day and you want to find the right places and the right times. As coaching becomes an *integral part* of your leadership style, you are always thinking about openings for coaching; what is the gap, what is the skill, what is the practice, and how can the team's performance improve?

"Openings" for Coaching

When we teach our *coaching leader* course, we help leaders be on the lookout for *openings for coaching*. Those are the moments where the *coaching leader* sees an opportunity for a "coaching moment." As you develop your coach's eye, you will start seeing openings for coaching everywhere you look! The most common openings for coaching are:

- Performance shortfall
- Breakdown of some kind
- Attitude or behavior not in alignment with stated values of the team
- Someone not performing up to their potential

Experienced *coaching leaders* have a knack for picking their time and knowing when to take the opening to coach and assist people to reach the next level of success.

Time and Place

Remember the old saying, *there's a time and place for everything*. While it is best to err on the side of being very active in your coaching, great *coaching leaders* are smart about when and where to coach. Too much of anything can overwhelm and annoy people. The brain has a limited capacity for learning, so do not overdo it!

As a rule of thumb you should be actively coaching on a *daily basis,* but make sure to pick the most *productive* coaching opportunities in the day. The most productive opportunities are:

- High payoff or cost to the organization
- A new skill you have been wanting the team to learn/ see in action
- A bad habit you have been trying to eliminate

One of the faults I see in leaders is not coaching, *letting too much time pass,* and then figuring the lesson has passed. There is a shelf life to coaching opportunities. If you see one of your key team members drop the ball or you see a great coaching moment, it is not helpful to point it out to them three weeks later. It is much more helpful in direct relation to the time you meet with them.

Obviously, if people are in meltdown, major crisis or under a lot of stress, it may not be the best time for coaching. But conversely, that does not mean you have to wait a week to coach them, you might wait an hour or a day.

Do Not Wait Because You Are Not Confident How the Coaching Will Turn Out

Undoubtedly, the number one thing I hear from leaders as to why they did not coach someone, even though there was an obvious opening for coaching, is the following: "I was not totally confident as to how it would turn out. I was afraid I would not do it (the coaching) right." Even as a Master Certified Coach, I am never sure how any coaching interaction is going to turn out. That is half the fun!

Every Coaching Interaction is an Opportunity to Sharpen Your Coaching Skills

If you were learning how to become a master carpenter, you would see every job as a chance to learn something new. It is the same in coaching. In fact each situation you put yourself in that really challenges you will only accelerate your development as a *coaching leader.* You might make a mistake or two, but we are not practicing to be heart surgeons here!

If you stay focused on individual and team *performance* and have a *genuine* desire to help people grow and succeed, people will want to work with you as you hone your skills. I probably made a rookie coaching mistake or two along the way, but no one ever lost their *trust* in my commitment to help them succeed. Trust is key. Trust in yourself and trust the *process* of coaching and you and your team will grow and succeed.

So let's look at when you might coach.

In the Moment

This is obviously the best kind of coaching. When we see this in the sports setting, we see a coach on the sideline saying something to the player right then and there because it is fresh in everyone's mind. In the moment coaching is great when it can be handled appropriately. You do not want to be doing in the moment coaching with someone in front of their peers. Most people do not like that. In the moment could be when you are having a meeting with your direct report and they are stuck on an issue. That is a great time to use the coaching process to solve the issue and identify some new practices.

After the Fact

This is a very common form of coaching. Professional athletes will review the game tape later and then identify what kinds of mistakes were made during the performance. Musicians in an orchestra might listen to the performance after the fact and then identify some new techniques or practices that would improve their performance. After the fact coaching is very popular and effective, but, do not wait too long to do it! There is something that some clients call an **"after-action review."** This is a great tool for coaching after a big project, presentation, or client event. Pull your whole team together and do an after-action review. In business, so often we are off to the next project and missing those learning opportunities.

Set Up Structures

What I mean by structures are one-on-one and team meetings, and regularly set coaching sessions. You could make it a part of your company's culture to have an "after-action review" after significant events. Those kinds of *structures* provide you and your team the opportunity to have coaching occur on a regular basis. We will talk more in Chapter Nine about how practice makes perfect, but structures are agreed upon times, places and processes that allow you to regularly engage in coaching.

It Doesn't Have to be Perfect

I can't emphasize this enough! Do not wait to start coaching until you think you know how to do it "just right." Trust the coaching *process*. Your early attempts at coaching will surprise you in their effectiveness. As successful business leaders your inclination will be to avoid being an unskilled novice. Fight that inclination! The only road to mastery is through the rocky roads of new skill building. Every coaching interaction will be building your experience, competence and confidence.

Consider hiring a coach to "coach the coach." That's me! Set up structures within your company so that you can have others be a second set of eyes and ears for you regarding how your coaching conversations went. Make some notes, practice being a detached observer, and you will get a sense of how you did in coaching.

In coaching school, we do three-way coaching. So you could even have a colleague sit in while you are coaching, or you could have a peer or even a teammate give you feedback about your coaching. The bottom line is, the only way you are going to become an effective *coaching leader* is to practice.

Breakdown Breakthrough

Every breakdown is a great opportunity for coaching and for a breakthrough. *Coaching leaders* see it that way. So certainly, every time there is a breakdown there is an opportunity for coaching. Remember, "time and place." Pick the right time and right place to coach around the breakdown. As an old saying goes, "In your greatest challenges, come your greatest opportunities." Always see breakdowns as an opportunity for coaching and a breakthrough.

A breakthrough can be one of those "ah ha!" moments where you see the light bulb go on. Your coachee is suddenly and permanently altered in a good way; they have a new perspective or new way of relating to someone or something.

David Rock Dance to Insight

In his book, *The Coaching With the Brain in Mind*, David Rock talks about the dance to insight. In the coaching conversation you will even see it in your coachee's eyes when they have the insight. Remember, in the PACE™ coaching process, it is a bit of a circular conversation that has some ebb and flow to it. None of this is going to occur unless you are practicing and engaging in the coaching conversation. There is nothing more rewarding than seeing the light bulb go on with your coachee. The more you coach, the more you will develop intuition about *where* the insights are waiting to happen. Don't overthink it. Just have the conversations and the process will take care of itself.

COACH THE COACH

As you reflect upon your inherent style, your beliefs, and your assumptions about your coaching skills, think about:

- Will you tend to coach too often or not often enough?
- Are you likely to hold back due to lack of confidence?
- Do you believe in the idea that every coaching interaction allows you to grow as a coach?

Identify any actions and perspectives you would like to focus on in relation to Chapter Eight, "Start Coaching and Keep Coaching."

CHAPTER NINE
Deliberate Practice for Results

Research Studies Prove *Practice* is the Key to Greatness

Since Professor K. Anders Ericsson of Florida State University's groundbreaking research in 1993, many scientists have been able to prove that practice is what makes some people better performers and produce the highest results. Research indicates that across a broad spectrum of activities, from medicine to performing arts to sports, people who are the very best at what they do practice more and practice differently than anyone else.

The research focused on something called *deliberate practice*. Deliberate practice has a few key characteristics:

- The practice is *detailed* about specific techniques
- The practice was designed to produce a very *specific result*
- The practice involved *stretching past your current capacity*

When I first read about the idea of deliberate practice, I thought it scientifically and empirically validated the very essence of coaching. As an Executive Coach, I have been focused on helping business leaders identify and practice the *specific skills and attitudes* they must master to become the best leaders they can be.

The deliberate practice idea also supported the notion that if these leaders could learn how to effectively coach their teams using deliberate practice, they would have a *proven recipe for competitive success.* The **coaching leader** idea now had the statistical support and evidence I needed to sway the logical, numbers-driven CEOs.

Let's Better Understand Deliberate Practice

Let's talk about regular practice versus deliberate practice. Let me describe my two different practices in golf and see if you can discern the difference.

In regular practice, I hit a large bucket of balls every week, thinking that this will make me a better golfer. In deliberate practice, I hit 100 golf balls with my nine iron, with the goal of hitting at least eighty of them within a ten-foot circle of a flag stick that is 125 yards from where I am standing. Do you hear the difference?

Do not forget my golf deliberate practice example as you help your coachees commit to new practices. Specific, detailed, and highly focused intended results are the very essence of both deliberate practice and greatness!

Phelps, Nash and Horowitz

These three men are great examples of practice at work. Most of us know about Michael Phelps, the Olympic gold medalist. His coach spoke on Good Morning America. He talked about how Phelps practiced 365 days a year. The news reporter asked the coach, "Did Michael practice on Christmas day?"

"Absolutely," his coached replied.

"On his birthday?" the interviewer asked.

"For sure, twice on his birthday."

Can you imagine? So, if you wanted to win a gold medal, you would learn from this conversation that you might have to commit to that level of practice. Now, not everyone has Michael Phelps' body type and not everyone has his muscle makeup, but the point is, of all the other swimmers who have similar body types and muscle makeup, his intensity and his commitment to deliberate practice obviously put him over the top.

Two time National Basketball Association All-Star, Steve Nash, is another example of the power of practice. Nash has one of the most reliable and smooth jump shots in the history of the NBA. Upon further investigation you learn he is *extremely regimented* in both his off-season practice regimen and his pre-game routine. Before every game, Nash shoots the ball from the same locations all over the court. During the game it looks easy, but his accuracy is the result of an unwavering commitment to disciplined practice.

Vladimir Horowitz was one of the greatest piano players of all time, and was quoted as saying, "If I stop practicing for a day, I notice it. Two days, my wife notices it. Three days, the critics notice."

If one of the best piano players on the planet had to keep practicing daily to stay at that level, what does that tell us about business and leaders? We have to keep practicing.

Bill Shover's Routine

Bill Shover, my Little League baseball coach, had a practice plan that was regimented and the same every time. As I look back now, I can see it was deliberate practice. We warmed up, threw balls back and forth, played "situation"(which was a mock game of baseball) which helped us be more prepared, had batting practice and then we ran.

That routine was the basis for learning the fundamentals and becoming very good at what we did. Dean Smith, the North Carolina basketball coach, and John Wooden, the UCLA basketball coach, were both legendary for their commitment to practice.

Never Stop Practicing

In his book, *Mastery*, George Leonard shares one of my all-time favorite quotes. Leonard says the Buddhist masters had a saying, "Before enlightenment you chop wood and carry water. After enlightenment you chop wood and carry water." The beauty of this message is that if you are to achieve and maintain greatness, it will require a lifelong commitment to practice.

In his book, Leonard teaches us to take joy in the very art of practicing. In the business world I believe there is a common belief that as a twenty-year veteran you've got it all figured out and you've arrived. I think when you look at Vladimir Horowitz, and you think about what Leonard is teaching in his book, you should actually see practice as the *destination*.

Eight-to-One Ratio

In the NBA, you practice eight hours for every hour you perform. In a business setting it seems like we don't give ourselves permission to practice and we don't understand why we don't keep getting better!

Identify the *Deliberate Practices* for Your Team

Now that we know about deliberate practice, the question becomes *what* should I be practicing in the deliberate practice sort of way? Only you and your team know what would be a *stretch past your current capacity*. Think about that and decide.

Let's take a page out of Bill Shover's coaching book and consider focusing on the *fundamentals*. Having worked with some of the most respected companies in America, I still see the need for building skill in the fundamentals. To me the fundamentals in business are:

- Interpersonal communication
- Collaboration and being open-minded

- Conflict resolution
- Time management
- Task management
- Commitments management
- E-mail management
- Self-management
- Emotional intelligence

This list gives you a comprehensive set of skills to work on; when you finish you can start right back at the top again.

Make Your Practice Plan

By now you understand that practice is the key to high levels of results. What is your practice plan? Let me make a few suggestions of typical business structures that could be good practice plans for you.

- Weekly staff meeting
- Weekly one-on-one meeting with direct report
- Monthly leadership team or all staff meeting
- Annual performance review
- Quarterly performance review
- After-action review on major projects
- Quarterly or semi-annual leadership offsite retreat (practice, NOT boondoggle!)

Every one of those meetings and structures is an opportunity to develop and implement deliberate practices for yourself and your organization.

COACH THE COACH

Think about your organization and your own personal work style and decide where and how you are going to instill the idea of practice in your organization.

Build your own practice plan in a detailed way. Cite the most common ways you will be practicing, including the length of time to practice, the skills you are building, and the people who will be involved.

CHAPTER TEN

Coaching—Real-Life Stories

Now that you have been immersed in the PACE™ coaching process, let's accelerate the learning by rewinding some of the game film from over the past ten years in my Executive Coaching practice. I have picked some of the more common and typical types of coaching scenarios in hopes that it will stir up your thinking and help you get a sense of how to use the PACE™ process in your own organization.

You will probably recognize some of these characters on your team, so take time as you look through each of the stories and think about how you might have approached the issue before and how you might approach the issue now as you coach people on your team.

In each scenario I am going to give you a little story at the beginning and at the end and, for the sake of efficiency, give you bullet points throughout each of the four steps of the PACE™ process.

Deaf CEO

Stan was like many of the CEOs I have coached over the years. Most CEOs did not get to where they are by being great listeners. They got there by being decisive, aggressive and prone to action. For many, like this particular CEO, the organization is not going to function without them until they learn to grow and empower others.

Stan's lack of listening skills was almost legendary in the organization to the point where it had become a significant source of frustration for most of his senior leaders. Stan had a stated objective of growing the next level of leaders, yet his inability to listen without stifling new ideas being discussed and acted upon was undermining his long-term vision. Here is what the PACE™ process looks like:

Perceived Need:

- Ability to listen to allow others to grow their leadership voice and impact in the organization.
- Increased respect for the CEO and his/her ability to demonstrate impact by more empowering, more facilitation, and less dictatorial rule.

Analysis:

- Self-observation—Become more aware of where, when, and why the lack of listening was occurring. In some meetings more than others? With some people more than others?
- Self-reflection—Did you really think all of your ideas were the best? What kinds of feelings and emotions do you experience when you are doing all the talking? What do you think the impact is on others in the organization in general when you do not listen to them? What message does it send?
- Other strategies or tactics? Perhaps give people permission to tell you to shut up. Give your senior executives permission to come up with a physical hand signal to remind you to talk less and listen more. Make a public declaration to your senior team to work on your listening skills.

Commitments:

- Begin practicing "mirroring back" what people say to you.

- Tell senior leaders to "call me on it" when I'm not listening.
- Make a public declaration of working on better listening skills.
- Ask for feedback from senior leaders in both individual and group settings with regard to improvement of listening skills.
- Set the goal to move talk/listen ratio from 90% / 10% to 25% / 75%.

Execution:

- Coach witnessed senior leaders call CEO on his behavior.
- CEO made public declaration of working on listening skills.
- Talk/listen ratio was dramatically transformed.

The results were excellent. Stan made tremendous progress and was acknowledged for his efforts from his senior leadership team. Respect for the CEO increased and his future successors were able to find and hone their leadership voices. I am happy to report that he has removed himself from the day-to-day business and is enjoying his role of Chairman of the Board.

Professor Monotone

Terry was a very well respected, technically brilliant senior leader in a technology company. Terry reached his position in the organization because of his ability to solve complex issues that faced the company. The problem now was that Terry had a growing reputation for spending too much time "pontificating" as he shared his wisdom with other members of the organization. To compound the issue, Terry's tone and communication style were very monotone, somewhat slow and always consistently steady.

The result was that people were not seeking Terry out to absorb his knowledge so that they could reach his level of technical expertise. Terry's value and stature in the company was beginning to fall as a result of his communication style. He could sense people pulling away and was concerned about his impact and future legacy in the organization.

Perceived Need:
- To be a highly valued and sought out leader in the organization.
- Learn how to employ "vocal variety" as a strategy to keep audience members engaged and interested.
- Increased self-awareness of lifelong patterns so as to change them.

Analysis:
- Self-observation—Keep a keen awareness of tone, body language, and vocal variety in dialogue with co-workers.
- Practice awareness about your own physical energy, exercise, and eating habits that impact physical energy.
- Begin experimenting with vocal variety as a means of keeping co-workers engaged in dialogue.

Commitments:
- Practice using vocal variety and a high level of awareness in every conversation.
- Practice at being spontaneous and a bit unpredictable in your interaction with others.

Execution:
- Reports from staff and peers showed dramatic changes in the communication style that resulted in being sought out by others.
- Terry enjoyed his work more and found the new communication style enhanced his engagement at work.

Terry is now noticeably different when engaged in conversations. His work at the office had a similar impact in the other areas of his life, including friendships and with his significant other. Terry is more spontaneous and sought after in all areas of his life. He feels a renewed sense of engagement in his career and a sense that he is both highly valued in the organization and will be remembered as one of their key leaders well after he is gone.

Fire Raging Out of Control

Jeff was a middle-aged, highly competent production supervisor for a mid-sized manufacturing company. He was incredibly passionate about the company but unfortunately his passion would sometimes turn to rage and verbal abuse directed at some of his fellow employees.

His contribution to the company's bottom line was huge, but his temper was becoming legendary and people were avoiding him. The CEO was contemplating terminating him.

Coaching oftentimes involves the use of behavioral assessments as another data point for understanding performance tendencies. One assessment we utilize measures Earth (Methodical), Wind (Extrovert), Water (Peacemaker) and Fire (Driver). Jeff was an extremely high Fire.

I said to Jeff, "You need to use your fire to light the way, not burn the village down!" I told him nobody wanted to be near him due to the scorched flesh they walked away with.

When I said that to him you could see one of those "ah ha!" moments. Years later he cites that as a pivotal moment in his development.

Perceived Need:
- Ability to make use of his drive and passion in a more productive and collaborative way.
- Self-control of his emotions.

Analysis:
- Self-observation—Noticing the moment when you are going to "burn the village down."
- Self-reflection—What other ways could you speak about your passion for the company that would inspire and motivate your co-workers?
- In what other ways could you burn your energy more productively?

Commitments:
- Practice taking three breaths before speaking.
- Practice speaking about commitments to quality rather than anger over performance.
- Be aware of your impact on others and check in with co-workers and apologize if you get angry.

Execution:
- Developed much better self-control.
- Learned to speak in ways that inspired commitment.
- Mended damaged relationships with key staff members.

Jeff made significant progress toward restoring his value in the organization. To be able to see him have that breakthrough and refer to it for years to come was one of my most rewarding coaching assignments. Those moments stick with you as a **coaching leader** *for the rest of your life!*

Verbal Floodgates
George was a well-intended, bright and knowledgeable Senior Vice President who had the unconscious and annoying habit of going on and on in his verbal interaction with others. The pattern was causing a decline of George's perceived value in the organization. Other executives were not including George

in certain collaborative sessions due to the issue. The CEO and board were beginning to lose confidence in George's chances of being promoted in the future.

Perceived Need:
- Ability to be more concise and articulate.
- Confidence and presence with executive level peers.

Analysis:
- Self-reflection—What is your internal dialogue when you were asked to give your ideas at the executive meetings?
- What other strategies could you use to become more concise and articulate?

Commitments:
- Deliberate practice—Write your key ideas down first and then practice forcing yourself to rewrite them until you get them under 500 words.
- Monitor and notice your nervousness with the executive team.
- Create new internal dialogue focused on self-trust.
- Get feedback from the CEO and give permission to be redirected.

Execution:
- More concise and articulate presentation of ideas.
- Enhanced confidence and presence in executive meetings.
- Become more respected among senior leader peers and board of directors.

The results were very positive. George learned to be more concise which resulted in higher levels of personal confidence. His practice of writing down his ideas first became one of his deliberate practices that he uses to this day.

Ms. Know It All

Emily was a very bright, highly competent Chief Financial Officer for a large technology company. She was so bright, in fact, that she could not stop herself in meetings with her fellow executives. She was always jumping in and telling them how they should handle their problems. This was becoming a significant source of frustration at executive meetings. Emily's working relationships with her peers were becoming distant and strained.

In our coaching sessions it became apparent this was a lifelong pattern for her. From an early age she felt she needed to prove to everyone how smart she was. Unfortunately, this strategy produced the same results at the last three jobs—they loved her brilliance as a CFO but hated the fact that she seemed to grandstand in executive meetings.

Perceived Need:

- Desire to think she needed to solve everyone's problems.
- Inability to stay in her functional area of responsibility.
- Lack of self-awareness of impact on others.

Analysis:

- Self-observation—Watch for patterns about when and why she wanted to jump in and fix it.
- Self-reflection—Think about why she had to keep proving her worth vs. having trust in her value without jumping into other's areas.
- Think of other ways she could contribute without appearing to grandstand.

Commitments:

- Practice self-awareness and self-control and not jump into solving other executive's problems.
- Practice asking questions that might help others solve their issues.

- Practice self-awareness and realize the impact you are having on those around you.

Execution:

- She was able to shut up in executive meetings.
- She was able to ask questions or contribute to others outside of group meetings.
- Gained awareness about seeing the impact on others in meetings.

Emily eventually started to be sought out by peers for her knowledge and ability to creatively solve problems. Her working relationship with peers improved and her value in the organization was appreciated.

Calm Down Tiger

Dave was a CEO who had reached a high level of success due to a high level of urgency, angst, attention to detail and drive.

Dave was wearing out himself and people around him. He got so worked up that he was having a hard time relaxing and disconnecting from work in the evenings. His wife came up with a verbal request, "Calm down, tiger." That seemed to work.

Perceived Need:

- Learn to unplug from business in the evening.
- Realize that not everyone is going to have your same level of intensity.
- Learn how to delegate to others and let them do it their way.

Analysis:

- Self-observation—Notice the conditions that cause you to get overly worked up.

- Self-reflection—What is it going to cost you (longevity/health/happiness) burning this much energy?
- What duties could you delegate to others?
- What other ways could you learn to unplug at night and on weekends?

Commitments:

- Practice saying to yourself, "Calm down, tiger" when you get upset.
- Bring examples of delegation to coaching sessions.
- Shift from being top producer to mentoring others.
- Enjoy a weekend at the ranch twice a month.

Execution:

- Was noticeably less angry on more occasions.
- Spent weekends at the ranch at least twice a month.
- Was able to distance himself from work and enjoyed a broader, long-range perspective.

Dave has made great progress. Guys like him know that it will take lifelong work and daily practice to stay calm. His drive and attention to detail is a great quality in so many ways, but if it drives him to an early grave, what is the point? I think Dave sees that perspective more often than not.

We See You At Your Desk, But Nobody's There

Tim was a successful senior manager in a large financial services company. The feedback during his 360-degree process (where we ask several people to tell the coach what the coachee does well and where there is room for improvement) was that he had a legendary reputation for "multitasking" during his one-on-one meetings with his direct reports. Furthermore, they reported that even though they would be talking to him, it was as if he was not present.

His direct reports were becoming increasingly frustrated with him and felt like they were not getting the support they needed.

Perceived Need:
- Ability to stay present and listen to direct reports.
- Self-control to not multi-task while others were in your office.

Analysis:
- Self-observation—Develop self-awareness about when and how you drift away as others are talking to you.
- Self-reflection—Think about how it must feel to be on the receiving end of your behavior. What impact is this having on your perceived value as a leader?
- What other strategies and tactics could you employ to mitigate these issues?

Commitments:
- Practice self-awareness about staying present with direct reports.
- NO multitasking of any kind when in the presence of others.
- Place BlackBerry out of reach on passenger's seat of car while driving.
- Get up and sit on the other side of the desk with direct reports when they come to talk to you.

Execution:
- Direct reports related a noticeable difference in staying present.
- No multitasking.
- Practicing "mirroring back" to demonstrate listening.

Tim's stock as a leader rose dramatically in the organization. His satisfaction in his job increased, he had more energy, and felt more organized by eliminating the multitasking habit.

Lone Ranger Workaholic

Pat was the CEO at a medium sized plumbing distribution business and one of the most committed, hard working, and attentive CEOs I had ever worked with. He had grown his business to become one of the most successful and respected in the region.

The problem was he did not know how to let go, work less, and let others carry the load. I would get e-mails from him starting at 5:30 in the morning with great ideas and questions about the coaching initiative we were undertaking in his firm.

While he talked about succession, it became apparent no one could do it as well as him. His key leaders were beginning to disengage because he would not delegate. His wife and kids wanted to spend more time with him.

Perceived Need:

- Unable to let go and delegate to others.
- Finding the right balance between work and family.
- Need bigger vision—legacy, company going on without him.

Analysis:

- Self-observation—Can you see opportunities to delegate to others?
- Self-reflection—What are you "getting" by being the hero in the company?
- What are the costs of this "do it yourself" strategy?

Commitments:

- Begin to delegate responsibilities to others.
- Bring concrete examples of delegation to your weekly coaching session.
- Leave work at 6:00 p.m. every evening.
- Work only one weekend each month.
- Begin two recreational hobbies—one with your spouse and one without.

Execution:

- Leave work on time.
- Seeing others take on responsibilities and succeed on their own.
- Begin to enjoy some outside hobbies.

Pat began to shape new behavior patterns that began to give him confidence in both his ability to let go and others' ability to succeed without him. The company flourished in a new way and his family got to see more of him.

Big Leader in a Small Body

Kim was a very successful Regional Vice President for a professional services firm. While she was well respected in the firm, senior executives noticed that at client events she acted very timid, not befitting her level of responsibility in the firm. Kim was short in stature and a bit intimidated at the larger group settings.

Her poor showing in group settings was seriously impacting her image with the top executives in the firm. This issue had the potential to stall a very long and successful career in the firm.

Perceived Need:

- Ability to project strong leadership presence in group settings.

- Ability to be outspoken and be seen as a thought leader in the firm.
- Ability to be confident with top executives in the firm.

Analysis:

- Self-observation—What was your inner dialogue at the large group events?
- Self-reflection—Notice when you start to withdraw, don't interact, and do not speak as much as you should.
- What other ways could you become more comfortable with top executives in the firm?

Commitments:

- Practice putting yourself in the front of the room more often, making key presentations at events.
- Research ahead of time and have a few key talking points with strategic ideas for the firm.
- Seek out top leaders in the room vs. waiting for them to come see you.
- Be aware of voice tone and volume, and practice stronger verbal projection and body language.

Execution:

- Received positive feedback from top leaders who noticed her stronger presence.
- Was sought out to speak at other events in different regions within the company.
- Had more confidence in seeking out top leaders at events.

This was a very satisfying coaching engagement to see this woman really blossom in her confidence and executive presence. She has continued to grow in her role and responsibilities.

Love to Battle

Joe was a highly competent leader in a customer service call center. His ability to manage the call center was excellent, but his relationship with his peer leaders and the CEO left a lot to be desired due to his unconscious need to "do battle" on just about any subject in the managers' meetings.

He later admitted that this behavior was what was valued and practiced on a nightly basis in his home growing up with several siblings. Many times in coaching we help people see old patterns that no longer serve them and create new patterns.

Perceived Need:

- Ability to stop doing battle with everyone.
- Self-management in meetings with peers.
- Need to mend relationships with CEO and peer leaders.

Analysis:

- Self-observation—Ability to catch himself two seconds before he was going to engage in another battle.
- Self-reflection—Think about the impact on his career and ability to provide for his family if the behavior continued.
- Think of ways to connect and re-establish good working relationships with peers and CEO.

Commitments:

- Practice catching himself and not engaging in battle.
- Practice looking for what was right about what the other person said vs. what was wrong about it.
- Learn to laugh at himself, not take himself so seriously, and be able to generate a more lighthearted persona.

Execution:
- Stopped automatically engaging in battles.
- Found areas of common interest with peers and CEO; began to build new and more productive working relationships.
- Learned to laugh at himself and not take things so seriously.

Joe slowly began to learn how to work more professionally. His interactions became more productive and rewarding. His value in the company became more in line with his outstanding contributions as the call center manager.

Hopefully these real life coaching stories and their PACE™ summaries help you get a sense of how PACE™ is applied to common, everyday performance gaps. You may encounter some of these personalities in your business.

CHAPTER ELEVEN

Eight Pitfalls That Will Undermine Coaching

Now that you have good coaching knowledge and techniques in your leadership tool box, I think it is time for a reality check. The most well intended and properly executed coaching will not overcome the eight pitfalls I have identified as coaching killers.

1. Can't Model

One of the most common problems I see is leaders who *espouse* certain values and beliefs, but they are not willing to be held accountable to their beliefs. The executive who says, "Everybody's equally important in this company," yet gives preferential privileges to himself and other members of the executive team. The CEO who says, "Integrity is a key component of the culture," yet talks behind people's backs.

You can put any pretty words you want on the wall, but if you are not able to set the tone and *be the example*, it will never work, period, end of story! It is not realistic to expect that you are going to be perfect 100% of the time—that is not what I am talking about. What I am talking about is an extremely *high level of integrity* and ability to *model* the values, and if at some point you miss the mark, be transparent with your team, apologize for your mistake, and recommit to the values. People can actually respect you more when you can demonstrate your vulnerability and be accountable for it.

2. Skill Versus Commitment

You can see when someone has a lot of commitment, but does not have the skill. In coaching this is one of our common diagnostic tools. Do I think this person really wants to do this or do they have the skill? Do not confuse the two. Furthermore, is the person able to *develop* the skill? If you decide they do have commitment, but they just do not have the skill, remember some people are not able to develop certain skills.

3. Keeping Poor Performers

One of the cultural contexts of our country is loyalty and fairness. Both of these are wonderful qualities, but in the ultra-competitive world of today, we may not have the luxury of keeping poor performers.

Say a person has been with the CEO from the very early stages of the company; they are now one of our most long-term and loyal employees, but for any number of reasons, their skill set and ability has not kept up with the complexity of the company or the competitive market. The company has tried to coach the person. They may have even tried reassignment, but this person is not able to perform at a level that is required today. It is time to manage this person out of the business.

4. The Uncoachable

What if one of your people is so stubborn and hard headed that they just won't be open to new ideas and new ways of doing things? I do not know why some people are so damn stuck in their ways. One of my first teachers said, "*Why* is a booby prize!" In other words, it is not worth looking for *why* people do certain things.

There are people I have come across over the years who just seem uncoachable. They are not open to new ways of doing things. For a while they will tell you that they are willing to change, and they will pretend like they are, but they never really commit to anything different. Do not waste your time coaching those people.

One test we use for this is "How hard am I working on the coaching?" If you are working a lot harder than the coachee, something is wrong. The coachee should be the one breaking a sweat!

5. No Patience to Allow Coaching to Develop: "It Takes Too Long" Attitude

I hear this complaint from a lot of leaders. I believe this is the wrong way of looking at it. Yes, it does take you a few more minutes to coach than it does to manage or to just do it yourself. Remember, coaching is about **building capacity in others**. The investment and time you spend on coaching should pay major dividends down the road.

Coaching is not a quick fix. It is a mindset and general philosophy about leadership and business. If you do not have the patience or fundamentally do not believe in coaching, do something else.

6. Overemphasis on Money

Some organizations talk about wanting to grow and develop people, but at the end of the day, all of the decisions seem to be made relative to finances and shareholder value. If we go back to the trust issue that we talked about early on, if people do not trust you they are not going to allow you to coach them.

When a company puts too much emphasis on finances, the coaching never feels genuine or takes hold.

7. Toxic Culture

Similar to overemphasis on money, in some organizations there are a variety of other, either historical or environmental issues, that make the place so sick that the coaching has no room to breathe, get integrity or take hold. These toxic cultures take on many different forms and usually are a result of toxic leaders. Toxic cultures are found where there may be addiction, abuse, dishonesty or epic political struggles. If you have a toxic culture, coaching is not going to take hold.

8. Misaligned Assistants

I have worked with organizations that have senior executives who are able to model the company's values, yet allow a few of their mid-level managers to act in ways that are not in alignment with company stated values. The most common reason for this is that the mid-level managers are technically excellent or produce high levels of financial results, but are unable to model the company's values.

You can see the slippery slope this creates for senior executives. This behavior sends the message, "We really believe in our core values and want everyone to follow them, but when it comes down to it, we are tolerating misalignment because certain people produce great (technical or financial) results and we are unwilling to draw a line in the sand." That is a recipe for disaster from a leadership standpoint.

Can These Common Pitfalls Be Overcome?

Just about any problem can be fixed, but these types of pitfalls require extraordinary focus, commitment, and probably dramatic upheaval to be overcome.

If you feel like your organization has some of the symptoms identified in these common pitfalls yet you are committed to becoming a *coaching leader* and creating a coaching culture, I would encourage you to bring all the heavy equipment you've got because you have an even bigger challenge ahead of you.

Consider bringing in a few more resources and employing some dramatic tactics to accomplish your goal. Just as a rocket ship needs "escape velocity" to get out of the gravitational pull of the Earth, your company may need help to overcome the strong gravitational pull of these pitfalls. This is not to say it cannot be done, but you ought to know what you are dealing with.

COACH THE COACH

Reflect upon the most common pitfalls and think about:

- Do you and/or your organization exhibit any of these common pitfalls?
- Do you think you don't have the exact pitfall, but you do have some traits that are close to these pitfalls?
- Are you being honest with yourself or kidding yourself about these pitfalls?

If you have even a *hint* of one of these pitfalls, or worse, have one of the pitfalls in your organization, list one to three actions you can take to mitigate or eliminate the pitfall.

CHAPTER TWELVE

Refining Your Coaching Voice

Values Clarification

It is gratifying to see how empowering it is for people to take the time to contemplate and declare their values. It is surprising *how little* people have actually thought about their values.

Most people live their lives and suddenly look around and see the values in action. While not a bad way to get there, imagine what you can come up with when you sit down and think strategically about the values needed in your business to help you succeed in the marketplace.

As you develop your coaching voice, it is imperative that you have the *guts* to put a stake in the ground around your values. The values set the backdrop for your team and your coaching messages. One of the most undermining things a *coaching leader* can do is to put their values on the wall in a pretty frame, yet act in direct conflict to the values.

As part of the process, after you have gained clarity on your own values, you should invite others on your team to either buy into those values or propose modifications that would include their own values. Remember, at the heart of coaching is creating **authentic commitment,** which only comes when people have choices. When a team of people buy into meaningful values they become more focused and committed to producing results.

As you think about values relative to business and leadership in your coaching, there are several things you might be thinking of:

- Speed
- Determination
- Customer service
- Excellence
- Quality
- Reliability
- Success
- Integrity
- World-class results
- Fun
- Creativity

Take a moment now and begin to get clear about what your values are. How do those values line up with your company's values? What do your values indicate about alignment with the people on your team and the people you are trying to attract to your team? There are no right or wrong values, so have fun. This will be an important backdrop of your coaching.

Famous Examples

Lee Strasberg is one of the most widely known and famous acting coaches. You really knew what you were getting with Strasberg. Strasberg's key values were commitment and intensity. He asked his actors to completely surrender their egos to their work. If you were not willing to do that, then you were not going to work with Lee Strasberg. He demanded great discipline of his actors, as well as great psychological truthfulness.

Elia Kazan, one of the most famous stage actors in the 1940s, wrote in his autobiography about Strasberg: "He carried with him the aura of a prophet, a musician, a witch doctor, psycho-analyst and a feared father of a Jewish home." Now that gives you something to shoot for as a coach!

Strasberg was the father of the method form of acting. So it wasn't necessarily right or wrong but it was Strasberg's approach. He has garnered some of the greatest respect and admiration of many of the best actors of our time. Strasberg was deeply impacted by Constantin Stanislavsky, when he brought his Moscow art theatre to the United States in 1923. As we look at most great coaches and their values, their approach, and their style, we find that they usually have their roots in another teacher. This is important as you think about the impact you will have downstream on your students.

Pat Summit, the women's basketball coach at the University of Tennessee, has the most wins of any coach in the NCAA (men's or women's). She is a known taskmaster, yet has developed an incredible reputation for the way she connects with her players as a role model and educator. She will be the first to tell you that her success (eight NCAA championships) is all about her play-ers. Now in her thirty-sixth year as the head coach, she has kept her team in the top tier of success for nearly four decades due to her willingness to continue to be a student of the ever-changing game of women's basketball. The Lady Volunteers Principles is a great example of her coaching values in action:

1. Respect yourself and others
2. Take full responsibility
3. Develop and demonstrate loyalty
4. Learn to be a great communicator
5. Discipline yourself so no one else has to
6. Make hard work your passion
7. Don't just work hard, work smart
8. Put the team before yourself
9. Make winning an attitude

    10. Be a competitor
    11. Change is a must
    12. Handle success like you handle failure

Vince Lombardi was probably the most famous coach in our American culture. He was the head coach of the Green Bay Packers from 1959 to 1967. Lombardi's values and coaching tenets are not only still alive and well, but you see them hanging in the offices of CEOs in corporate America to this day. Vince's values were:

- Hard work
- Strength
- Determination

Probably his most famous quote is, "I firmly believe that any man's finest hour, the greatest fulfillment of all that he holds dear, is that moment when he has worked his heart out in a good cause and lies exhausted on the field of battle—victorious." So if you are going to be on Vince Lombardi's team, you better be tough and willing to sacrifice yourself for the good of the team. Lombardi's teams won championships and were feared and revered by everyone in the league. He had such an impact that to this day the NFL championship trophy is called the Lombardi Trophy.

Lombardi's determination and grit even boiled over to the point where he got himself in trouble. He said that you should hate your opponent as if you wanted to kill him. As a devout Catholic that statement caused Vince a lot of grief and he later recanted a bit. The bottom line was that you had to be tougher then your opponent.

John Wooden was another one of the most famous coaches of our time. Wooden was the head basketball coach for the UCLA basketball team from 1960–1977. Wooden's values can be conveyed in one brief story.

Bill Walton, one of the greatest basketball players of all time, tells the story. "In my first meeting with Coach Wooden, he asked me to come into his office and I looked forward to getting some of the finest pearls of wisdom of the greatest mind in basketball. Coach Wooden said, 'Show me how you tie your shoes.' I thought to myself, *What the hell are you talking about? I thought I was going to be getting some of the greatest wisdom of all time.* He was serious. He asked me to lace up my basketball shoes."

Wooden said to Walton, "This is one of the first things I want you to know. This is how we tie our shoes around here. And we do it the same way every time. Do you understand kid?" Coach Wooden went on to explain that if you don't lace up your shoes correctly it can lead to blisters, which can lead to injury and lost playing time and could cost the team.

Later, Bill Walton laughed and explained how astonished he was by the attention to detail on the fundamentals. This was John Wooden's focus and approach: attention to detail down to the smallest, most mundane things, such as lacing your shoes. Bill Walton got a sense of this man from the very first meeting. If Wooden was strict and regimented about lacing up the shoes, imagine how he was on every aspect of running a basketball team? Wooden believed if you focused on the fundamentals, the rest would take care of itself. They ended up with nine championships to prove it.

Pete Walsh

My coaching values are:

- Reaching your potential
- Continuous improvement through practice
- Being in the top 5% of our field
- Enjoying working together

The value of continuous improvement through practice was born in my driveway, shooting basketballs. It later turned into regularly scheduled meetings with my warehouse and delivery staff. It became a permanent value when the research about **deliberate practice** came out in the past decade.

The value of being in the top 5% was probably born out of being raised in a competitive society, but more importantly, it is a great benchmark to push toward. In my previous profession (office furniture) and my current profession there are industry associations that track results by a wide variety of measures—number of clients, revenue, number of employees, top line revenue, bottom line profit—that can give you a way to track the top 5% goal.

The goal of enjoying our work together is rooted in two places. First is the little kid in me who really enjoys having fun. I have a picture of myself as that ten-year-old boy on my desk as a daily reminder. Second is the real life experiences I have had of seeing how much gets done, with less struggle, by people who really like and enjoy each other. Conversely, teams that are made up of people who really do not enjoy being together find ways to hide behind rules and policies to not work together. Life is short; you ought to enjoy the people on your team.

Creating Your Unique Coaching Stand

Now that you have thought about your values and the values of some of the greatest coaches of all time, consider your industry and demographics. It is time for you to develop your unique coaching stand. What is it going to be? Remember, there is no right or wrong answer. As time goes on, you get older, your industry evolves, and it is very possible that your unique coaching stand will evolve with the times. My observation has been that with Lombardi and others, some of the very strong underpinnings of their style actually did not change over time.

The sooner you can frame up and understand your unique coaching stand, the sooner you will be able to use that as a backdrop for all of your work. Remember, one of the ways people develop trust is through consistency. So the more you can understand and know your unique coaching stand, the more you can deliver on a consistent basis. An exercise at the end of this chapter will help you reflect upon and reframe your coaching stand.

Bill Shover's coaching style was about practicing the fundamentals and having a good time. We had a process called "situation" that we engaged in in every practice session. I came to find out later that Shover's style was impacted by one of the greatest coaches of the twentieth century, Tony Hinkle. He was a man who coached three sports at Butler College for more than forty years. Hinkle was legendary in his approach and style. Hinkle believed that if you practiced something enough times it would become second nature to you and to your muscle memory, so that when the situation arose in the game setting, you would simply react. I can now see Hinkle's thinking and Bill Shover's "situation" drill and I can tell you firsthand—it works. There is no reason you cannot take the same type of approach in your business.

So, Shover got his approach from Hinkle, I got my approach from Shover and who has gotten their approach from me?

COACH THE COACH

Sit down and reflect upon how you would like to be remembered as a coach. Think about the top values and attributes that are most meaningful to you and that you would like people to remember about you twenty-five years from now. Perhaps think about those coaches and teachers in your life that had the greatest impact on you. What qualities did they possess? Are those the types of qualities you would like to portray to your team members? What qualities are most needed in your business or your profession?

Come up with five to ten key attributes that you would like to be defined by as a coach. Reflect upon how, as a *coaching leader,* those attributes in action impact your business.

Begin to put those attributes into action in your coaching leadership tomorrow.

CHAPTER THIRTEEN

Enjoy the Journey

Ups and Downs

One of the most admirable and useful qualities of a great *coaching leader* is *resilience*.

Coaching, performance, and business results are all going to be full of ups and downs. Do not allow yourself to get too high or too low. Most great coaches have experienced both.

You will serve yourself, as well as your team members, if you learn how to stay *consistent* and true to your values and *focus on the fundamentals* at all times. That consistency and determination will provide great inspiration to your team.

Changes in the Environment

Many times changes in the environment will cause a huge impact in your ability to coach. I have been in three economic downturns in my career all of the greatest coaching in the world is not going to change certain economic conditions. Great *coaching leaders* know that and realize they should stay the course, stay true to their vision, continue working on the fundamentals and practicing, and acknowledge that changes do occur in the environment.

The most focused and fundamentally sound teams prevail even in extremely difficult conditions. Think about it from a football perspective. When it snows or rains, the teams that can still block and tackle are the ones that win championships.

Be Adaptable—Make the Most With What You Have

That had to be Bill Shover's philosophy when he inherited the Bad News Bears. As far as I could tell, Bill thought he had a group of talented ballplayers. I am sure he had to be creative about fielding the best team with all of the varying degrees of talent he had to work with.

Smart *coaching leaders* realize they may have to modify their core philosophies a bit and be adaptable at times. Take Arizona Cardinals Coach Ken Whisenhut as an example. It was widely known that Whisenhut wanted to turn the Cardinals into a *rush first* style of offense, much like the Pittsburgh Steelers, where Whisenhut had coached and won a Super Bowl.

Whisenhut was trying to make Kurt Warner, one of the greatest quarterbacks ever to play the game, conform to Whisenhut's run philosophy. After a few less than impressive games, Warner pleaded his case to Whisenhut and convinced him to temporarily set aside his run first philosophy due to the fact that he had one extremely talented passer. Whisenhut changed direction and reoriented the offense around Warner's arm and experience. Within two years the Arizona Cardinals made their first Super Bowl appearance in franchise history!

Surprise and Disappointment

That is part of the territory of coaching. There are going to be moments when you are elated and surprised at what some people can achieve and those will be some of your greatest moments. Conversely, there will be moments when you are shocked and disappointed when talented and committed people miss the mark and come up short. It is all part of the coach's journey and to be expected. You will appreciate the highs even more because you will have remembered the pain of the lows.

Trust the Coaching *Process*

I have been amazed over the years that if I stay true to my process, magical results happen even when I might think, "This time, coaching may not work." If you have the right intention and pay attention to each step of the process, I promise you, people's results and commitment will improve.

The Merrill Lynch Story

There was a very senior executive at Merrill Lynch who was at his retirement party. A large number of his peers gathered at his house. They got up one after another and told great stories of the man's courage, tenacity, and success in business. They each talked about how great he was and all he had accomplished.

His eighteen-year-old daughter stood up and said, "I'm so glad to hear all of you share about my father, because truthfully, I really don't know him." Around the room tears welled up in many of those executives' eyes. Suddenly they realized that while they all had huge successes and had conquered enemies on the field of battle, they had perhaps missed one of the most important accomplishments in their lives!

Be a great *coaching leader.* Produce great business results. Find balance in all that you do. Growing people is very rewarding but it's not the *only thing.* Balance is one of life's fundamentals.

Don't Forget About Significance

Let's go back to what Coach Holtz said in his book: "Coaching is an opportunity to be successful long after you're gone." Regardless of your type of business, coaching is simply a means of applying your talents, making a nice living, and hopefully, making an impact in this world. But if you can become a great *coaching leader* you can impact those around you, which could in turn impact others that you don't even know, many years down the road.

Start Your Own "Coaching Tree"—You Never Know How Big It Will Grow

Imagine for a moment how many lives Tony Hinkle impacted not only through his forty-one years of coaching three sports at Butler College, but then through Bill Shover's 334 young men. Shover's 334 men, who like me, most likely went on to coach their own kids' Little League teams. We worked on fundamentals, and it was *THE GREATEST* time of my life; hopefully those kids will grow up and coach their kids in the Hinkle/Shover approach.

Not to mention, one awkward kid on Shover's team who would go on to coach hundreds of CEOs and leaders, who impact thousands of employees in business, generating millions of earnings, as well as personal and professional fulfillment. How cool is that?

Jump in. Start your own coaching tree and plant some of Lou Holtz's seeds of wisdom.

Thanks for being open to the coaching!

#14 Was My Favorite Number

When it became apparent this book was going to be thirteen chapters, it seemed like such a bummer that I could not find a way to get to my favorite jersey number—#14.

To this day when I attend a niece's or nephew's sporting event I immediately look for old #14 to see who has the honor of wearing that prestigious and meaningful number. It takes me back to many fond memories.

Rather than just make up another chapter to get to fourteen, I thought you might enjoy (and indulge me in) a moment of nostalgia!

Pete 1974.

This is what Bill had to work with!
Talk about a coaching challenge and opportunity!

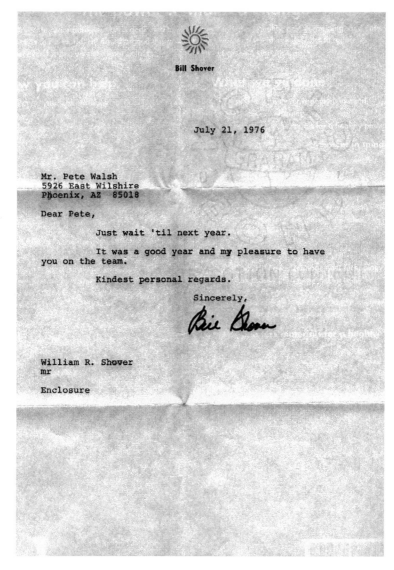

Bill Shover's end of year letter!

What a professional! Notice how a great coach keeps you motivated and looking forward to next year? I didn't rest on my laurels and assume he would draft me next year. I had better keep practicing in the off-season!

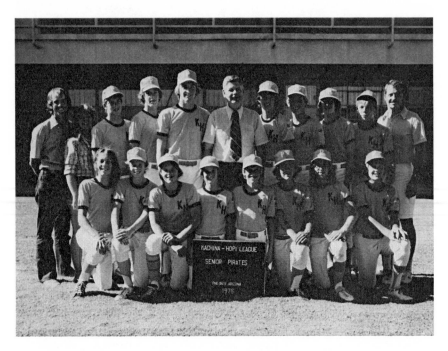

We are in the seniors now so I guess Bill figured he better wear a tie! He was probably working the day of this picture. His daughter Lisa was a regular around the dugout. That's me on the bottom row third from the right.

Rocky Coyle is back row right. Rocky was an unbelievable hitter and catcher and went on to play baseball professionally spending a few years in MLB's farm system. It makes you realize just how few kids get to the big show.

In 1977 several guys missed picture day! I'm sure we had more players than this. Here I am again, front row left—nice of Bill to allow the long hair! T.A. Shover in the front row center. From the looks of this photo and my recollection, T.A. was about 75% of this team. T.A. was a great humble guy then and still is today!

Still helping me 20 years after baseball! Speaking at my Rotary Club in 1997 sharing stories about Phoenix history, the Arizona NFL Super Bowl Committee and a few little league stories!

CPSIA information can be obtained
at www.ICGtesting.com
Printed in the USA
FFOW02n1902280114
3316FF